The Wisdom of Nature

Werner Telesko

The
Wisdom of
Nature

*The Healing Powers and Symbolism
of Plants and Animals
in the Middle Ages*

Prestel
Munich · London · New York

Cover: *Spring* (detail), see p. 47
Back cover: *Violet* (detail), see p. 43
p. 1: *Mandrake* (detail), see p. 44
p. 2: *Quinces* (detail), see p. 29

© Prestel Verlag
Munich · London · New York, 2001

Library of Congress Control Number and
Die Deutsche Bibliothek – CIP –
Cataloguing-in-Publication-Data are available

Photographic credits: see p. 95

Prestel Verlag
Mandlstr. 26 · 80802 Munich
Tel. +49 (089) 38 17 09-0, Fax +49 (089) 38 17 09-35

4 Bloomsbury Place · London WC1A 2QA
Tel. +44 (20) 7323-5004, Fax +44 (20) 7636-8004

175 Fifth Avenue, Suite 402 · New York, NY 10010
Tel. +1 (212) 995-2720, Fax +1 (212) 995-2733

www.prestel.com

Prestel books are available worldwide.
Please contact your nearest bookseller
or one of the above Prestel offices for details
concerning your local distributor.

Translated from the German by Stephen Telfer, Edinburgh
Edited by Christopher Wynne

Design by Kluy & Kluy, Berlin
Lithography by LVD, Berlin
Printed and bound by Westermann Druck Zwickau

Printed in Germany on acid-free paper

ISBN 3-7913-2585-X

Contents

INTRODUCTION

The Lord has created medicines from the earth,
and a sensible man will not disparage them.
(Ecclesiasticus 38, 4)

The Natural World and Medicine in the Middle Ages

The medieval understanding of the natural world must be seen in the context of a society in which religion played a crucial role. According to medieval thinking, nature was an open book in which God revealed both himself and his message. An educated person was called upon to read this work in which nature was seen as the embodiment of the Godhead and its expression. Following Psalm 148 and the song glorifying the Creation in Daniel 3, the whole of nature is often described in poetry in praise of the Creator. Day and night are symbols of good and evil, while spring reminds us of Christ's resurrection and the changing seasons signify the transient nature of human flesh. In literature, the changing seasons are frequently interpreted symbolically. Sedulius Scotus (mid-9th century), the head of the Irish colony of Liège, associated the gloom of winter with the absence of his benefactor, Bishop Hartgar of Liège, while the joy of spring was associated with his return. Many medieval poems entreat nature to share the pain felt by their authors; a frequent metaphor for the barrenness of the earth. Often in medieval literature, threatening natural phenomena are to be understood as symbols prefiguring political events or expressing nature's grief over slain heroes (as in the *Song of Roland*).

Even in antiquity nature was attributed with a wide range of functions: as the creator of the world, the mother and father of all

Fig. 1 Austrian National Library, Vienna. Ms. phil. gr. 2, sheet 1r; illuminated initial in Aristotle's Physics

things, the sculptor of the earth, places and people, the force that brings order out of chaos and the provider of mankind. These views later found expression in numerous book illustrations such as in the illuminated initial in Aristotle's *Physics* from the end of the 15th century (fig. 1) in which Nature sustains the earth with her milk.[1] This creative process is equally strikingly depicted in a miniature from Burgundy dated between 1487 and 1504: Natura has almost finished creating a child on her anvil – one leg is still missing. The grey colour of the prototypes lying on the ground on the left of the picture identifies them as being 'prefabricated' models (fig. 2).[2]

The love that the Middle Ages had for the plant world is apparent in the descriptions and illustrations of monastic gardens. Indeed, the 'garden' (*hortus*) may be regarded as the concept at the centre of monastic thinking. Besides the kitchen garden, a flower garden is also usually mentioned. Apart from medicinal and herbal plants, other essential items in monastic gardens were plants of great religious symbolism such as the madonna lily and the rose (pp. 38, 40). Many plants were sown for their healing powers and used in monastic dispensaries. Charlemagne, for instance, in his inquiry into the administration and husbandry of Frankish lands – *Capitulare de villis* (795) – decreed that roses, lilies, rosemary, scilla, iris, sunflowers, poppies, common mallow and marshmallow were to be grown on every farm.

Monks were considered to be especially skilled in the art of healing. By copying the manuscripts of the medical writers and physicians of antiquity, they helped preserve the thoughts of the great authorities on medicine – Hippocrates, Dioscorides, Galen of Pergamum and Celsus – until the foundation of Europe's universities. Important medical treatises, such as the herbals by Dioscorides and Pliny the Elder, were summarized by Dark Age scholars such as Walahfrid Strabo (808/809–849), Abbot of Reichenau, whose *Hortulus* was written in the 840s.

The role of plants in salvational history is a fundamental one. In the Christian version, the Fall turned man into a frail, ill and mortal being. The model of salvation to be followed by doctors was that of Christ the physician, *Christus medicus*. Using his medicines, a doctor, nature's 'partner', is not only able to restore the balance of the cardinal humours, but can also encourage his patients to lead a life that is well-pleasing to God. Earthly medicine thus takes on greater significance as a route to heaven. According to Arnald of Villanova (1240–1311), a teacher at Montpellier medical school, the Almighty created medicine and it serves man's every need. It was, he said, not only a means to maintain health, but also a way to perfect a life. Hildegard of Bingen (1098–1179), the founder and abbess of a convent at Rupertsberg near Bingen on the River Rhine, also assumed that God's power was to be found in the latent forces of plants.

The use of vegetable preparations was only one method of medical treatment possible in the Middle Ages. In the hierarchy of treatments envisaged by the renowned bishop and scholar Isidor of Seville (*c.* 570–636), three therapies are described in strict order of application: dietetics as a way of life, pharmacy as pharmacology and surgery as 'intervention with an armed hand'.

Herbals and the 'Tacuinum sanitatis'

Ever since prehistoric times, humans have used animal, vegetable and mineral substances to cure sickness. Herbals, books containing the names and descriptions of plants, are not medical treatises in the narrow sense, although pharmacopoeias were still comprised mainly of vegetable-based drugs during the life of Paracelsus (1493–1541). This was why a physician still needed at least some knowledge of officinal plants. In antiquity it had mainly been the drug collectors and root hunters (*rhizotomoi*) who were concerned with the preparation of that most important source of drugs.

Medicinal plants can be applied externally as a balm, ointment or plaster and taken internally as potions, powders, syrups, oil, pills or an electuary. The medicines used during the Middle Ages were mostly compound preparations, i.e. mixtures of various substances that were sometimes also treated chemically. Most preparations, either as pastes, potions or ointments, were less complicated to make than the legendary *mithridate* whose use was the preserve of kings. It was not uncommon for physicians to practice simultaneously as apothecaries; this enabled them to dispense their own medicines.

A papyrus from around 400 AD may claim to be one of the oldest extant medical illustrations. Unearthed in 1904 at Antinoopolis in Egypt, it was named the 'Johnson Papyrus' after its discoverer. It may be assumed that the majority of medical books in ancient Greece and Rome were illustrated, unlike those compiled during the Middle Ages when most treatises on *materia medica* were not. This suggests that the knowledge required to classify plants was passed on orally for the most part or was gained by direct observation of the plants themselves and less by academic study.

Between the 3rd century BC and the 7th century AD, Alexandria was the foremost centre of medical research and training, yet its vast collection of medical papyri has been lost, as have the details the papyri might have supplied about the origins of medical illustrations. For whom were manuscripts containing medical illustrations produced? What role did they play in everyday medical practice? There are no easy answers to these questions because the manuscripts often bear only their owner's name and give few details about how they were used.

Hellenistic and Byzantine works containing numerous elements of folk medicine may be considered the principal sources of many herbals. The most important ancient exemplars for authors in the Middle Ages were the herbals of Crateuas, physician to Mithradates VI of Pontos (1–63 BC), of Pseudo-Apuleius (*Apuleius Barbarus* or *Apuleius Platonicus*, *c.* 400 AD) and of Pedanios Dioscorides from Anazarbus in Cilicia (first half of the 1st century AD), a military doctor under Emperor Claudius (41–54 AD). Dioscorides's main work, *De Materia Medica*, was translated into many languages including Anglo-Saxon, Provençal, Persian and Hebrew.

The plant illustrations in the original Latin version of Apuleius's herbal may have been based on even older copies. Scholars have studied the various versions of Pseudo-Apuleius and have identified southern Italian, German and Anglo-Norman manuscript categories whose influence lasted into the 13th century. While Crateuas arranged his herbal alphabetically, Dioscorides in his five-volume pharmacological study attempted a proper classification of around six hundred plants, trees, roots, herbs, aromatics, oils, ointments and minerals.

Fig. 3 Austrian National Library, Vienna. Codex 93, sheet 61v; Homer, the healer and Hermes with the legendary herb moly

Dioscorides's *De Materia Medica* was highly respected and was praised by Galen of Pergamum as the most perfect of its type and was often copied during the Middle Ages. While the work was originally conceived to have text only, attempts were soon also made to illustrate the plants discussed in it. This gave rise to the difficulty of identifying some of the plant illustrations by their botanical name because the miniaturist very often did not know what individual plants looked like. This not inconsiderable difficulty would occupy minds in the future and is exemplified by the illustration of the legendary herb *moly* in the famous Dioscorides manuscript[3] held in Vienna. The miniature has large, brownish flowers although they are described in the text as white and smaller than those of the violet. This particular manuscript contains illustrations of plants that do not quite tally with the natural form and some appear even to have been invented. The names of many preparations are based on ancient traditions, have etymologies going back to pagan times and often make use of the names of gods from antiquity.

The legendary herb *moly*, moreover, is a particularly good illustration of the origins of pharmacology in ancient mythology. It is mentioned in Homer's *Odyssey* in which Hermes presents *moly* to Odysseus to protect him from the spells of the enchantress Circe. In the relevant miniature from a codex in the Austrian National Library, a 13th-century collection of ancient medical wisdom (fig. 3), the poet Homer is shown on the left.[4] The central figure is that of the healer (*archiater*), seen turning towards the poet, while Hermes, with a plant in each hand, stands on the right. Botanists nowadays are unable to say with certainty which plant *moly* is, but it may be *Allium Moly*. The accompanying text states that the plant is used to ease pain in the womb. Another example of the mythological origins of plants in manuscripts by Pseudo-Apuleius is the *Herba Artemisia*, said to have been discovered by Diana who passed on knowledge of its useful properties to the centaur Chiron (fig. 4).[5]

Fig. 4   Bodleian Library, Oxford. Ms. Ashmole 1462, sheet 18r, Herba Artemisia

The Viennese Dioscorides manuscript, like *De Materia medica*, is arranged alphabetically; each picture – there are 383 full-page illustrations on sheets 12v to 387r – is accompanied by texts after Dioscorides, Crateuas and Galen of Pergamum and is shown alongside rows of variant spellings of each plant's name, mainly after Pamphilos. This famous manuscript, commissioned before 512 by residents of Constantinople's Honoratae Quarter for Juliana Anicia, the daughter of Olybrius, the western Roman emperor in 472, was still being used by physicians in the 16th century. It contains splendid plant illustrations from late antiquity in two different styles: some are Hellenistic miniatures that almost have the character of nature studies[6] (fig. 5); others are greatly simplified and schematic with no spatial depth to them[7] (fig. 6). The writings of Dioscorides were not restricted to Europe; *De Materia Medica* also reached the Islamic world in an Arabic translation from the Greek made by a Christian resident of Baghdad around the year 854.

Between the 5th and 10th centuries, numerous copies were made of Dioscorides's herbal and Pseudo-Apuleius's Latin herbal. There may, indeed, be far greater continuity between the Hellenistic period and the Middle Ages in the history of illustrated herbals than in other types of medical illustration, although the naturalistic quality of the illustrations in the Viennese Dioscorides manuscript was not achieved again until the 15th century. Illustrations in herbals

Fig. 5 Austrian National Library, Vienna. Codex med. gr. 1, sheet 29v; (Arnoglossen)

Fig. 6 Austrian National Library, Vienna. Codex med. gr. 1, sheet 194v; (Kestron)

often not only show the plants themselves, but place them visually in the context of a story that is intended to portray their effects.

Besides scenes showing aggressive dogs, snakes and scorpions, there are also illustrations that combine images of the encounter and the bite or sting with an image of the physician offering a curative potion extracted from the plant in question. Such images of physicians 'treating' their patients which largely make use of the readers' and viewers' everyday experiences and are not specifically scientific in nature, can include other figures and even in a miniature can depict several types of treatment by the physician. One such example is an illustrated sheet in a manuscript in Oxford's Bodleian Library (fig. 7); dated around 1200; its upper section shows a physician treating a patient's eyes, while the lower section shows another physician examining a patient's nose.[8]

The more often plants were copied, the less realistic they became – especially in illustrations of Mediterranean flora that did not grow north of the Alps and with which the miniaturists were unfamiliar. There is, for instance, a noticeable loss of realism in the plant illustrations in the miniatures in the above-mentioned 13th-century codex in Vienna, presumably originally southern Italian or Sicilian, that is essentially based on the Dioscorides manuscript. The 13th-century miniaturist did, admittedly, choose to make his illustrations substantially different by incorporating images of towns, physicians treating patients, dramatic encounters with poisonous animals, mythical beasts and mythological beings like centaurs and genies.

Besides the Pseudo-Apuleius group, a new generation of books describing healing substances developed during the 13th century. These books were based on texts translated from the Arabic and described new substances and prescriptions. The earliest known exemplars of an illustrated manuscript of the *Tractatus de herbis* date from the first half of the 14th century and were produced in the

Fig. 7 Bodleian Library, Oxford. Ms. Ashmole 1462, sheet 10r; physicians 'treating' their patients

13

southern Italian region of Puglia. These books clearly break with the visual style of Pseudo-Apuleius in that they reveal the first signs of a deliberate return to the observation of nature. The herbals produced north of the Alps had changed over time and no longer fulfilled their original purpose of allowing the physician or herbalist to identify the plants that he sought, and instead had become abstract and stylised. A manuscript of the *Liber de Simplici Medicina* (*Secreta Saler-nitana*), a type of dictionary of drugs, was written in Salerno in the early 14th century[9] and its miniatures reveal radical changes. The illustrations forgo long-established models in favour of the close observation of nature. One particular manuscript miniature combines a large image of the common houseleek (fig. 9) with a scene showing a man wielding a pick-axe while quarrying for sulphur near a town.[10] Sulphur itself was less important as a medicinal substance than sulphur flowers (sublimed sulphur), obtained by refining crude sulphur. It was used in numerous prescriptions during the Middle Ages as a laxative and expectorant or as a sudorific. In obvious contrast to the rigid pictorial conventions of Dioscorides and Pseudo-Apuleius, the close attention to detail and leaf shapes (fig. 8)[11] is accompanied by a change in composition – in other words an illustration of a plant can sometimes take up a whole page.

Jacopo Filippo, a monk from Padua, wrote a famous herbal around 1390–1400 at the behest of Francesco Carrara II, the head of the town's ruling family. He was removed in 1403 and was strangled three years later in a Venetian prison. The herbal associated with his name is an Italian translation (*herbolario volgare*) of an Arabic work by Serapion the Younger (around 800 AD) and is renowned for its accurate detail and colouring.[12] With its delicately shaded colours, intricately drawn

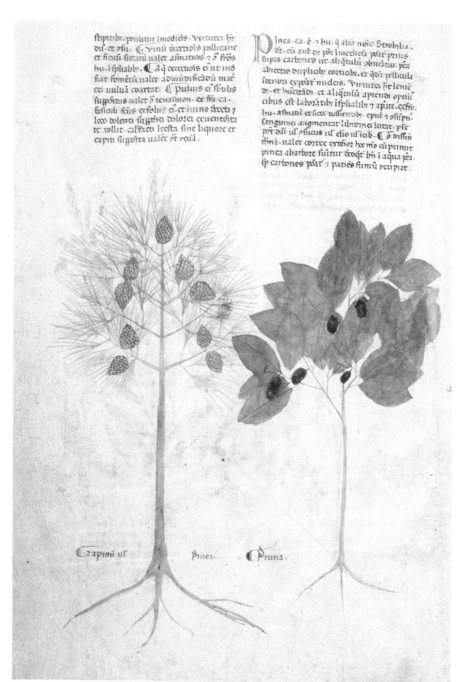

Fig. 8 The British Library, London. Ms. Egerton 747, sheet 74v; pine and plum

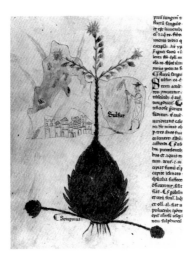

Fig. 9   *The British Library,
London. Ms. Egerton 747,
sheet 88v; common houseleek*

mença quanto se uen secca ne seche jnso pumo grado ouere jnso pm
cipio del seçondo. e siba pm uertu de abstergere çoso li humou che noln
la sostancia del molon ne quella del cogombaro. ¶ Diascoude ecadio
scriue che la sostancia del molon fa molto ounare. E quanto la si pestie
metua jn mucelo de uno empiastro suso li ogi sana le apostemation

Fig. 10   *The British Library,
London. Ms. Egerton 2020,
sheet 161v; melons*

veining, shading and different stages of development, the gouache drawing of the melon plant (*melones*, fig. 10) is unmistakably the product of a meticulous observation of nature.[13] It is apparent here that the artist was more concerned with precision rather than botanical classification. The manuscript's drawings are highly distinctive in that they break with the tradition of portraying plants in their entirety, as was generally the custom at that time (fig. 11);[14] instead plants are depicted freely and asymmetrically and taken diagonally across the page (fig. 12).[15]

The fundamental importance of this manuscript, held in London, during the transition to a new perspective on botanical illustration, namely one that was based on the close study of nature,

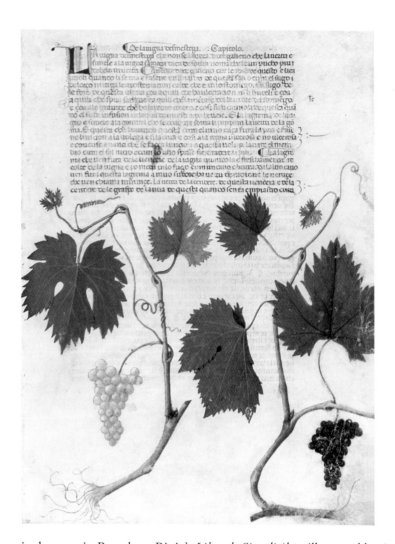

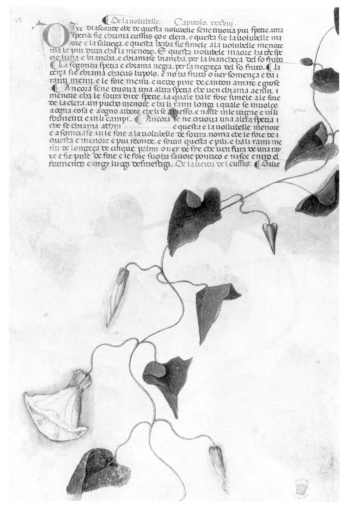

is also seen in Benedetto Rinio's *Liber de Simplicibus*, illustrated by Andrea Amadio in 1419. At least twenty of its five-hundred full-page illustrations are copies of pages from the Francesco Carrara herbal.[16] Rinio was a physician whose text was based on many of the authorities of antiquity and the Middle Ages and he also introduced some otherwise unknown plants.

A book of plants that was made around 1500 in northern Italy shows how, once the development of 15th-century illuminated herbals had run its course, the botanical and analytical representation of plants could be included in a scenic context, as exemplified by a hunting dog uprooting a mandrake (fig. 13).[17]

The text of the Paduan *Herbolario volgare*, held in London's British Library, leads up to the tradition of the Arabic *tacuina*, manuals in which the characteristics of individual plants are reduced to a minimum. The roots of the *tacuina* are to be found in the Greek physiology of the four bodily fluids (blood, phlegm, yellow and black bile) as developed into a homogenous system by Galen in his treatise *On the Natural Faculties* and furthered in the Middle Ages by Hildegard

Fig. 11 The British Library, London. Ms. Egerton 2020, sheet 28r; vine

Fig. 12 The British Library, London. Ms. Egerton 2020, sheet 33r; bindweed

of Bingen. In these terms, health can be said to be a balanced mixture of the fluids, ill health an imbalance. The emphasis of this genre shifts from a textbook-type presentation to lavish illustrations that show the importance of plants in everyday life. Moreover, the *tacuinum* manuscripts mark a change in the importance and function of plant illustrations. Some of the 15th century's loveliest flower paintings are found not only in herbals, but also in florilegia, in the marginal illuminations of manuscripts, in sketchbooks or in drawings by artists such as Pisanello, Jacopo Bellini, Leonardo da Vinci and Albrecht Dürer. Examples of 15th-century panel painting show that the gardens portrayed in them contain all the plants that Saint Albert the Great (*c.* 1193–1280), in his *Libri de vegetabilibus*, had earlier described as essential for a medieval garden. Depictions of herbs and plants in symbolic relationships, especially in the context of the iconography surrounding the Virgin Mary in Early Netherlandish painting, refer back to the great tradition of the symbolism of flowers during the High Middle Ages, as expressed in particular in 12th and 13th-century cathedral sculpture.

Fig. 13   Bayerische Staats-bibliothek, Munich. Codex icon. (bot.) 26, sheet 59r; mandrake

Tacuinum sanitatis

Tacuinum is an Arab word (*taqwim*) with a Latin suffix. *Taccuino* in Italian means notebook or pocket diary. The Arabic equivalent for *tacuinum sanitatis* is *taqwim es-sihha*, *taqwim* meaning 'tabular overview', *es-sihha* meaning 'of health'. The original format is related to these definitions. The *tacuinum sanitatis* is a table of correspondences based on the humoral pathology of the ancient world. Listing 280 items, mostly foodstuffs, it describes their positive and negative effects on the human body. Besides foodstuffs, the effect on human health and well-being of other things such as scents, the seasons, winds, types of clothing, accommodation, physical exercise, pleasure, etc. are also classified. The items in the original manuscript were listed according to subject matter as they are again in the illustrated manuscripts. The result is a comprehensive work that goes well beyond the specific character of a herbal – one that answers many questions about health and lifestyle. Often it is not the plant itself that is the focus of attention, but the human activity associated with it, for instance harvesting (p. 48). To enliven this list of plants, the miniaturist included representative figures from different social strata. Of the 206 miniatures in the Viennese manuscript,[18] only four contain no images of people. This is typical of the art of the time in which everyday activities were important subjects for illustrations.

The manuscripts give the author's name, slightly different in each one, at the start of each introduction. *Ellbochasim de baldach*, *Elluchasem elimithar* and *Albulkasem de Baldac* (p. 24) are, for example, all transcriptions of *Abu'l Hasan al Muhtar ibn al Hasan ibn Abdun ibn Sa'dun ibn Botlan*. This physician was a supporter of Nestorian Christianity and studied in his hometown under Ibn et-Taijib who died in 1043. Ibn Botlan practiced as a physician before 1047 in Aleppo where he appears to have become a Christian before his death in 1064. Of his *Taqwim es-sihha*, nine Arabic manuscripts have survived; of the Latin translation, seventeen codices are extant. The first Latin translation dates from the second half of the 13th century and the first printed version was published in Strasbourg in 1531. A German translation appeared as early as 1533.

Several manuscripts of an abridged version of the text are known to exist and contain more than 200 miniatures.[19] The Viennese manuscript Cod. ser. nov. 2644, containing 109 vellum sheets, was produced before 1405, the year it came into the possession of George of Liechtenstein, Bishop of Trent (*d.* 1419); his coat-of-arms is displayed in the manuscript. The codex, the property of the house of Cerruti, now known as *The Cerruti Housebook*, is not the oldest exemplar of this manuscript group. It is safe to assume that the client who commissioned the Viennese manuscript, produced either in Lombardy, or more probably in Verona towards the end of the 14th century, knew the version now in Paris (Ms. lat. nouv. acq. 1673). The miniaturist of the Paris *tacuinum* basically saw life from a courtly perspective and lent even the simplest task a hint of aristocratic elegance, while the emphasis for the miniaturist of the Viennese manuscript clearly lay in reproducing images of daily life. The illustrations in this manuscript group probably originated in the workshop of Giovannino de'Grassi (*d.* 1398) who is said to have greatly influenced the rise of the 'international Gothic style'. They even prefigure the naturalism that was to develop at the beginning of the 15th century.

What is odd about these manuscripts is the way the illustrations take precedence over the text. The brevity of the text and its continuous narrative, however, underline the importance of the images. The texts describing the individual miniatures follow a certain structure with regard to their content:

1. Every object has a *complexion* or 'nature' in the four categories of hot, cold, wet or dry and from the first to the third 'degree'.
2. *Electio* refers to the individual parts of a particular object that should be used first.

3. *Iuvamentum* describes the benefit to health derived from a particular object.

4. *Nocumentum* describes the harm done to one's health.

5. *Remotio nocumenti* describes the prevention of such damage by means of appropriate antidotes, administered either preventatively or to aid recovery to injuries already sustained.

6. *Quid generat* refers to the effect a substance has on the human body.

7. *Convenit* refers to a substance's suitability according to a person's temperament, age, the time of year and the location it is used in.

The content and objectives laid out in the *tacuinum* are based on the medicinal treatises of the Greek physician Hippocrates for whom balanced proportions of the fluids of the body were important. The human body, according to him, is composed of the four elements and their respective qualities of hot, cold, wet and dry. Things of a 'cold and wet' nature are beneficial to people of a warm temperament, e.g. for cholerics, as they are said to have a cooling effect and moderate the inherent predominance of one particular bodily fluid. This results in a harmonious balance that is the secret of good health. These categories show that a particular item is analysed as comprehensively as possible. It should be remembered that the original text was from the Orient and considers Arabic habits prevalent in Antioch, Aleppo and possibly Baghdad. The Italian artist had to rely on his imagination when depicting oriental flora but one result of the creation of an Italian version was that many peculiarities, customs and habits of Italian life – making macaroni, roasting chestnuts, or the hanging of garlands between trees – found their way into the miniatures.

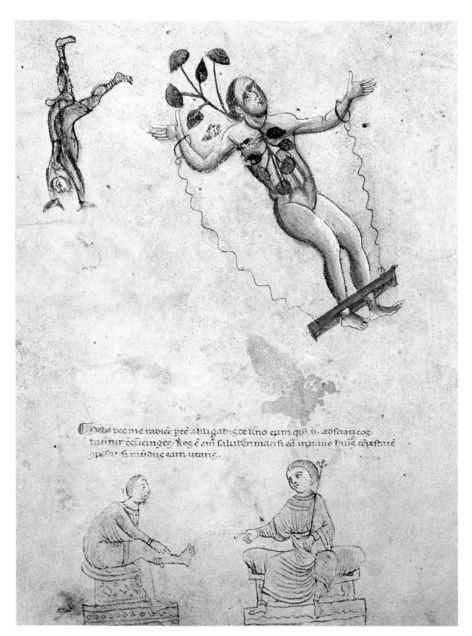

Fig. 15 *Austrian National Library, Vienna. Codex 93, sheet 72v;* Herba Paeonia

The task given to the miniaturists of the Viennese manuscript was to create faithful depictions of the smallest details from life and this approach resulted in the manuscript being wholly dominated by genre scenes. What is important is that the miniaturists were unable to resort to obvious models and schemes, but had to depend on the direct observation of nature and daily life.

The significance of the advice given in the *tacuinum* manuscripts was perpetuated mainly in the popular theory of the four temperaments. At the root of many ideas is the ancient belief in the 'signature' of the plant world, according to which the very shape of medicinal herbs suggests what they should be used for or what they should be used against; bryony, for instance, is recommended as a treatment for dropsy because it has the appearance of a swollen human leg. This so-called 'sign theory', much admired by Paracelsus, posits a divine plan of salvation in which man has been chosen to decipher the codes of nature.

Passages in the herbal of Pseudo-Apuleius that attribute some plants with miraculous medicinal powers can also be categorized as popular belief. One such example is *Herba Diptamnum*; wild goats or deer injured by huntsmen are miraculously healed when they eat it (fig. 14).[20] In the case of humans, such popular belief can result in some strange procedures in which plants become talismans, for instance when a plant is affixed to the patient. Thus the peony (*Herba Paeonia*) was said to protect sleepwalkers when tied around their necks (fig. 15).[21]

Empirical science in the modern age could not work with *medicina antiqua* and for this reason naturopathy was a major bone of contention. However, because it identified and portrayed the wider connections between the treatment of illnesses, the *tacuinum sanitatis* has been accorded an important historical and cultural place in the intellectual life of Europe.

Physiologus

Not only the large mammals depicted in bestiaries were regarded as sources of medicinal cures; quite a number of small mammals, reptiles and insects were, too. These animals were usually drawn without much attention to detail because they belonged to the lowest order of animals in the Creation. In contrast to the herbals, the medical books on animals have largely been ignored despite the fact that, compared with herbals, numerous works have survived, among them books by Nicander (*Theriaka*), Dioscorides (Book II of *De Materia medica*), Sextus Placitus (*De medicina ex animalibus*) and a Latin and Greek anonymus. The work by Sextus Placitus, *Papyriensis* (5th century AD), describes medicines obtained from animal substances. In the Latinized western world during the Middle Ages, the tradition was continued in the eminent Salernitan work *Circa instans* (around 1150) and in the Arab world by Ibn Buktishu's animal book. Other types of illustrated animal books are encyclopaedias, bestiaries and fables.

The Greek *physiologus*, probably dating from the 2nd century from Alexandria, is the model followed by all later bestiaries and was illustrated from the very beginning. Written by an anonymous author, it initially comprised forty-nine chapters and was widely available in Latin translation from the 6th century at the latest. Its fame came through a number of different versions. The *physiologus* was hugely popular early on but was often substantially changed. Four Greek editions are now recognized as forming the basis of Latin versions.

The *physiologus* is a Christian interpretation of the zoological knowledge of antiquity and explains nature in metaphysical, moral and mystical terms. This type of religious instructional literature was intended to give the simple believer an understanding of Christianity's rudiments through an explanation of natural objects. Unlike animal fables with their fictional plots (e.g. talking animals), the tales in the *physiologus* are accounts of natural conditions, although these were soon recognised by St. Augustine as scientifically mistaken. Their allegorical interpretations of nature frequently have only tenuous links with biological fact. What is said of the stag, for instance, is applied to the elephant (p. 82) because their Greek names are very similar (*elephas – elaphos*). The descriptions in the *physiologus*, written in the present tense to stress their relevance to contemporary readers, are thus not so much pertinent to living creatures as symbols that can be variously interpreted along Christian and mythical lines. The *physiologus*, which like almost no other allegorical piece of writing was held in the highest regard until the Renaissance, was used primarily in schools as well as for the spiritual instruction of clerics.

The oldest surviving illustrated Latin *physiologus* is the so-called *Bern Physiologus*[22] that may be based on a version from late antiquity. It was written in Carolingian minuscule by a monk called Haecpertus (Egbert); an entry on sheet 130r, HAECPERTUS ME FECIT, suggests that he may also have illuminated it. Produced around 835 AD at Hautvillers Abbey, near Reims, the centre of manuscript illumination under archbishop Ebo (in office 816–835, 840–845), the codex originally contained 136 sheets, of which 131 have survived. The manuscript is based essentially on the Latin *physiologus* and contains thirty-five chapters; each animal has at least one illustration and sometimes more than one. The manuscript exemplifies the artistic efforts of the Carolingian *renovatio*; the thirty-five miniatures with their pastose colouring and, in some cases, imaginative borders, are of varying formats and are inserted before each chapter.

Bestiaries

Bestiaries are collections of animal stories of a religious or moralizing nature that lend useful support to theological statements. Bestiaries developed after the Latin versions of the *physiologus* underwent substantial changes in scope and interpretation.

The term *bestiarium*, meaning 'book of animals', may have become established at the beginning of the 12th century. Quite large numbers of illuminated bestiaries have come down to us, mostly of English and French provenance, although many Italian, Catalonian and Castilian ones have also survived. The pinnacle of bestiary production was reached in 13th-century England. Illuminated bestiaries were first widely circulated in the 12th century and remained popular well into the 15th century.

The oldest French bestiary has much in common with the Latin *physiologus*; the Anglo-Norman poet Philippe de Thaon composed its thirty-eight chapters between 1121 and 1135. The bestiary produced by Gervaise at the beginning of the 13th century has twenty-nine chapters and 1,280 lines. The longest rhyming bestiary in Old French, with thirty-five or thirty-seven chapters, was composed around 1210–11 by the Norman Guillaume Le Clerc, while the most interesting French bestiary is probably that of Pierre de Beauvais from around 1218. The *Bestiaire d'amour* by Richard de Fournival, from the second half of the 13th century, represents a completely new interpretation of the traditional animal fable, albeit one that found no imitators, in which the animals are described in the style of courtly love poetry. The division of the *physiologus* into chapters describing and interpreting an animal is largely retained in the bestiaries. Not all the animals described and illustrated in the bestiaries were real, of course, although numerous attempts were made to identify such mythical creatures with living animals.

As with herbals, there is no standardised canonical text for bestiaries; variations extracted from early Christian and Middle Age texts are also to be found. The most important sources, especially of English bestiaries, are the early Christian *Physiologus*, St. Augustus's *Enarrationes in Psalmos*, the textbook *Moralia in Job* by St. Gregory I, the *Etymologiae* of St. Isidore of Seville, the *Hexaëmeron* of St. Ambrose, the four-volume tract *De bestiis et aliis rebus* from the 12th century, Hugo of Folieto's *De avibus* (after 1152), the *Collectanea rerum memorabilium* by Solinus (early 3rd century) and, less frequently, Peter of Cornwall's *Pantheologus* from the 12th century.

Almost half the miniatures in the manuscripts of bestiaries depict single animals within a frame and with no narrative. Narrative images, on the other hand, sometimes comprise several miniatures located in a rustic setting or set against an architectural backdrop. Allegorical miniatures may well be considered the most interesting. Their interpretations of the animals often go beyond the scope of the text and are placed alongside explanations of Biblical events.

1   Österreichische Nationalbibliothek (Austrian National Library), Vienna. Ms. phil. gr. 2, sheet 1r.
2   The British Library, London. Harley manuscript 4425, sheet 150r.
3   Österreichische Nationalbibliothek, Vienna. Cod. med. gr. 1, sheet 235v.
4   Österreichische Nationalbibliothek, Vienna. Cod. 93, sheet 61v.
5   Bodleian Library, Oxford. Ashmole manuscript 1462, sheet 18r.
6   Sheet 29v (*Arnoglosson*).
7   Sheet 194v (*Kestron*).
8   Bodleian Library, Oxford. Ashmole manuscript 1462, sheet 10r.
9   The British Library, London. Egerton manuscript 747.
10 Sheet 88v.
11 Sheet 74v (Pine and Plum).
12 The British Library, London. Egerton manuscript 2020.
13 Sheet 161v.
14 Sheet 28r (Vine).
15 Sheet 33r (Bindweed/Bearbine).
16 Biblioteca Nazionale Marciana, Venice. Cod. Lat. VI 59.
17 Bayerische Staatsbibliothek, Munich. Cod. icon. (bot.) 26, sheet 59r.
18 Österreichische Nationalbibliothek, Vienna. Cod. ser. nov. 2644.
19 Österreichische Nationalbibliothek, Vienna. Cod. ser. nov. 2644 and Cod. 2396; Bibliothèque nationale, Paris. Ms. lat. Nouv. Acq. 1673 and Ms. lat. 9333; Biblioteca Casanatense, Rome. Ms. 4182; Bibliothèque municipale, Rouen. Leber manuscript 1088 and Bibliothèque de l'Université, Liège, Ms. 1041.
20 Österreichische Nationalbibliothek, Vienna. Cod. 93, sheet 70r.
21 Österreichische Nationalbibliothek, Vienna. Cod. 93, sheet 72v.
22 Burgerbibliothek, Bern. Codex Bongarsianus 318.

THE PHYSICIAN AND HIS STUDENTS (Ellbochasim of Baldach)

The first miniature in the Viennese codex shows a scholarly physician talking to his students. It is an idealized image of Ibn Botlan (cf. p. 18), presented here in the tradition of an author portrait (one of the four Apostles) from late antiquity to the Middle Ages. The physician is seated beneath a baldachin behind his writing desk and is conversing with two students who are approaching from the right.

The text accompanying the miniature discusses human health and the benefits and harm associated with certain types of food, drink and clothing. A list of the factors determining the significance of the objects with which humans surround themselves follows. The text makes clear – also with regard to the work as a whole – that the *Tacuinum sanitatis* is not a rigorously scientific work, but that it is rather a compendium of dietetic advice for the benefit of lay persons with an interest in medicine.

"We shall also mention what each person should choose depending on his temperament and age and shall present the information in clearly-structured tables because the endless talk of wise men and the many contradictory, wise sayings contained within books often enough serve only to confuse readers. For readers want no more from science than effective help, not findings or definitions. Therefore it is our intention in this book to cut down on long-winded talk and to forgo different manners of speaking.

We also intend, however, not to hold opinions contrary to the advice of our predecessors who have spoken the truth. In this book we have contributed nothing other than the structural summaries, the concise answers to those who question, and proof, to reinforce the value of what has been said. Neither do we want to observe the designs of people who are different depending on the interpretation of their opinions.

We therefore call on God to guide our understanding as human nature alone is hardly free from error. May all our explanations indicate our modest good will and God give us strength in our resolve and help us as he sees fit."

PROLOGUE
The physician proclaims the rules of life.

*Austrian
National Library, Vienna.
Cod. ser. nov. 2644, sheet 4r*

Tacum sanitatis i medicina. ad naranou ser res neccias. uparraticé uiuaniti cibori 7 potuum.
7 iduntorum nocumiti ipium. Et i remotice nocumitorum uir oseclla meliori er antiquis-

Ilacuinusanitatis de ser reb3 q̃ sunt necc̄ cuilib3 boni ad cotidiani c̄suac̄ōe3: saitatis sue eu
suus recti fiet opationib3. Q̃rima é sparatio aeris/qui cor̄ contingit. C̄Scd̄a retificatio
cibi 7 pot C̄Tertia retificatio mot̄ 7 quietis. C̄Quarta phirbitio. corporis alsopno. 7 uigiliis mͦ
tis. C̄Quinta retificatio laxationis 7 o̓strietō̄is humor̄ C̄Serta regulatio p̄sc̄ i moderatō̄e
gaudu. uel tiͦmoris. 7 angustie/h3s eñ mͦis equalitatis erit c̄suatio sanitatis. Et remotiͦo
istoru ser. ab hac qualitate/ facit egrͦitudinē deo p̄mittite. glͦo se7 altissimo 7 sib̄ quolib3 gͦñe
sunt plures sp̄es 7 plimum necessͣe/ quaru dicem̄ nͣs/ si deo placuit. C̄Dicem̄ etiā electiͦ͠es
c̄ueiͦeͣntes cuilib3 sͫn c̄plec̄: 7 etiͦrē ipius/7 hec omnia ponem̄ i tͣbul/eop multiloquia sa
pientum qz fastidiunt auditores. 7 d̄uisitas multoru librͦorum opp̄oitoͣru. homines nͦo

Sour Pomegranates, *Granata acetosa*

As in other miniatures from the Viennese manuscript, the tree bearing the fruit described in the text is the focus of attention, combined in this case with the image of a lady richly-clad in a red cloak. She is shown putting pomegranates into an already full basket. In the centre of the foreground, a hare is seen eating a pomegranate with another two black-and-white hares shown in the left half of the picture. Two birds are sitting in the tree's branches, one of them picking at a piece of fruit. The hares symbolise fertility and are clearly linked with the pomegranate that the Romans called *malum granatum*, i.e. 'many-seeded apple', because of its multiple pips. This is how the pomegranate came to be interpreted as a fertility symbol. In botanical terms, however, the pomegranate has nothing in common with the apple, but is instead related to the myrtle family; besides the fig, olive tree and vine, it was one of Israel's main cultivated plants. Another type of pomegranate, the sweet pomegranate, *Granata dulcia*, is depicted in the Viennese codex on sheet 7r but can barely be distinguished from the sour pomegranate.

While the pomegranate in antiquity was associated with beauty, blood, fertility and immortality, in Christian symbolism it came to represent Christ's death and resurrection as well as the life-giving virtue of the Virgin Mary and her many qualities associated with the Redemption.

As a symbol of the Salvation, the Christ child in 15th and early 16th-century Italian paintings of the Virgin Mary holds a burst pomegranate in his hand, exposing its red inside, a reference to Christ's blood, and its many seeds. Another interpretation again associates the pomegranate closely with the Church: the many seeds contained within its skin symbolise the large number of saints and the red colour refers to martyrdom.

The manuscript text explains that sour pomegranates, eaten when juicy by someone of a 'cold complexion', are very good for the liver. The fruit can harm the chest, however, but this danger can be avoided by eating dishes sweetened with honey.

Sour pomegranates produce moderate nutrients and are especially suitable for people of 'warm' nature, adolescents, in summer and in warm climes. Even early on, it was believed that to eat three small blossoms from the pomegranate tree would prevent eye trouble for a whole year.

Symbolism
Symbol of fertility and marriage; the virtues of the Virgin Mary.

Medieval Medicine
Aids the liver, protects against eye complaints.

Medicinal Effect
Pomegranate skins used as an anthelmintic.

Austrian National Library, Vienna. Cod. ser. nov. 2644, sheet 7v

Granata acetosa.

Granata acetosa. ꝑplo.fri. Acetō q̃ sunt multe sucositatis. iuuantur epi ca. ꝯfer. nocuitiũ nocent ꝑectori. Remo nocuiti cum calce melito. Quid gn̄arit˙ chimum˙mo dicum. Mag̃ ꝑueniũt calis. iuuenibꝫ eftate. cale regioni·

QUINCES, *Citonia*

The miniature portraying the quince is typical of most of the botanical illustrations in the Viennese manuscript. Like many of the other images, this one does not focus solely on the fruit; the real charm here arises from the juxtaposition of the flora and the company of the nobleman and the two women. The young man in the strangely ornamented court dress on the left-hand side of the picture and the two elegant ladies on the right, all dressed in long, pleated and ample robes, are shown picking quinces and enjoying the fragrance of the fruit.

The plant cultivated in Europe originated in western Asia, Arabia, the eastern Mediterranean and Crete from where it takes its name (Cydonia). The quince tree is small but produces large, yellow, pear-shaped, squarish and ribbed fruit, with a very hard flesh, that mature in late autumn. Quinces are rich in pectin. The mucilage surrounding the seeds has emollient and soothing properties. When cooked, the fruit makes fines jellies and preserves. Quince syrup soothes hoarseness and throat infections, is anti-diarrhoeal, but in large doses is also purgative. Nowadays the seeds are used only in cosmetics. Country people often make preserves, jellies and syrups using quince and take its coated seeds to treat skin burns and inflammation of the eye.

The text below the miniature describes the qualities and effect of the quince whose complexion is cold and dry in the second degree. It has a positive effect because it pleases the heart and stimulates the appetite. The quince can, however, be a cause of colic which can be prevented by eating sweet dates. In addition, the text states that quinces have a cooling and harmonising effect and are, therefore, particularly suitable for choleric types. Having eaten many quinces during pregnancy, women are said to give birth to diligent and quick-witted children.

MEDIEVAL MEDICINE
Pleases the heart and stimulates the appetite; good for pregnant women.

MEDICINAL EFFECT
Rich in pectin, soothes burns, sore throats and inflammation of the eye.

Citonia.

Citonia. ꝯplo. fri. ꞇ ſic. in ꝛ. Electio ꝯpleta groſſa. iuuami. lerificat ꞇ ꝯfortat apetitu. nocumᵗ
cauſat colicaᵣ. Remoᵒ noxti eū dactiˡ melitis. Quid gñat huioᵣeᷓ fri. ꞇ uenuit mag colicaᵣ
. omni etati. omni tṗᵉ. omni regioni.

PUMPKINS, *Cucurbite*

Many fine examples of the large bottle gourd (*Cucurbita lagenaria L.*) are seen hanging among foliage in one of the most interesting miniatures in the Viennese manuscript. In the foreground a man and a woman are busy harvesting the pumpkins and placing them in a basket.

Walahfrid Strabo (808/809–849), the abbot of Reichenau, commented extensively on the pumpkin in his *Hortulus*: "Growing from a common seed, it provides strong shade with its shield-like leaves and forces its tendrils into the dense branches…".

Spanish seafarers brought the pumpkin to Europe in the 16th century. To be certain that the fruit will grow as large as possible, its seeds have to be planted while the biggest church bells are being rung; the pumpkins, so it is said, will be as big as the bells! Numerous uses for the pumpkin are mentioned in old herbals, for instance it can be used to treat liver disease, inflammation of the kidneys, bladder trouble and other internal diseases. Pumpkin seeds were popularly used in folk medicine to treat tapeworms and roundworms and are now used to cure an irritable bladder as well as general bladder trouble and inflammation of the prostate gland. The seeds are also effective at the onset of the enlargement of the prostate gland leading to an obstruction in urine flow. For women, stewed pumpkin was thought to prevent vomiting during pregnancy.

The text accompanying this miniature describes the pumpkin's complexion as cold and wet in the second degree and that the fruit is best eaten when fresh and green when it quenches thirst. The problem with the pumpkin is that it quickly acts as a laxative, but this can be overcome using salt water and mustard. In addition, pumpkins are said to be good for choleric types, adolescents, in the summer and can be enjoyed everywhere, but especially in southern climes. To grow an especially large pumpkin, a seed should be removed from the centre and planted pointing downwards in the ground. Menstruating women should be kept away from pumpkins because they could prevent it from growing.

MEDIEVAL MEDICINE
Aids in cases of liver disease, inflammation of the kidneys, bladder trouble and internal diseases.

MEDICINAL EFFECT
Relieves bladder trouble and inflammation of the prostate gland.

Austrian National Library, Vienna. Cod. ser. nov. 2644, sheet 22v

Cucurbite. cplo. fri. a hu. l. î ꝉ. Electio recetes uuidæ. uuamj tum mitigant. sitm No
cumitum. cito lubricant. Remo nocumiti. cu muri ꞇ sinapi. Quid gnat? mutritnu
medici ꞇ fri. Suenuit colicis iuuenib; estate. omib; regioib;ꞇ ꝓꝓue midionatb;.

BASIL, *Ocimum citratum*

The miniature shows a man placing a basil plant in a large red and blue, two-handled, earthenware vessel. Found in all tropical and subtropical regions, this twenty to fifty-centimetre tall bush contains ethereal oils and tannins. It has been cultivated for thousands of years in the temperate zones of the Mediterranean, but reached western Europe only in the 16th century. A plant that grows especially well in warm and sunny locations, fresh basil leaves have a slightly sweet, peppery aroma. Dried basil is widely used as a kitchen herb.

Basil is one of garden herbs not found in the wild and is a labiate that was known in antiquity. It is mentioned in early Sanskrit writings where it is called *arjaka*. In India it is dedicated to the Hindu gods Krishna and Vishnu. Basil wreaths have also been found in Egyptian graves. *Basilikon* means royal, while *basileus* is the Greek for ruler. In ancient Rome basil was prized as a herb and a medicinal plant. During the Middle Ages, it was used to drive out evil spirits and 'dragons' and to treat depression as well as heart complaints and stomach trouble. Basil sap was used to treat ear inflammation, among other things, and was also widely used as an antidote for snakebites. Basil was frequently associated in the Middle Ages with scorpions that were believed to spend a lot of time near the plant. Taken with wine and vinegar, it was said to be helpful in counteracting scorpion bites. Basil was also considered good for the stomach, to assist digestion, to be a cardiotonic, to cleanse the uterus and to induce labour. Basil sap cleans the intestine and produces accrid bodily fluids. Moreover, it is said to have a nerve-strengthening and clarifying effect.

In southern Europe, basil is placed in pots in front of houses to keep flies away. Although nowadays it is rarely used as a medicinal plant, it is still mixed with tea to cure flatulence or an upset stomach. It is now a popular herb that adds a sweet and fiery flavour to vegetable dishes and butter. Other species of basil are also cultivated. *Ocimum minimum* is a miniature variety that grows only fifteen centimetres high. *Calamintha clinopodium* is a related species that grows in northern Europe with a fragrance and flavour reminiscent of thyme.

SYMBOLISM
Sacred to the Indian gods Krishna and Vishnu.

MEDIEVAL MEDICINE
Drives out dragons and evil spirits, helps cure snakebites and scorpion stings; clears the intestine.

MEDICINAL EFFECT
Rich in ethereal oils, aids digestion, used as a spice.

Oçimum citratum.

Oçimum citrini. ↄplo. casa in g. sic. in p̄. Electio bn̄ odorifex. uumitus. es sba stigit
sic laxat uentrem. Nocumtum. obtenebrat uisus. Remotio. nocumiti. etī poztulaca. Qd̄
gñia ↄt humorez. acutum ↄ inflatiuum. Juenit fris. scib; breme ↄ septentonalib;

MINT, *Menta*

This miniature depicts a garden in which two women, one older, the other younger, are collecting mint leaves (*Menta piperita L.*, peppermint) in a basket.

According to Greek mythology, the nymph Minthe was transformed into mint by Persephone. Various mint species were known in antiquity and were used in medicines by the Egyptians, Israelites and Romans. The Egyptians and Greeks also added mint to their beer and used it in beauty care. Charlemagne's *Capitulare de villis* (795) and the famous plan of the monastery at St. Gallen (around 820) recommended the cultivation of several mint species.

In place of smelling salts, mint is said to have an invigorating effect on someone who has fainted. Mixed in pomegranate wine, it cures hiccups and nausea. The liquid obtained from the whole plant in a distillation flask is described as an effective cure for nose bleeds. Milk does not curdle, so it is said, if a few mint leaves are dropped in it. Peppermint tea is used to treat diseases of the respiratory tract and digestive organs. Peppermint oil or menthol is applied externally as an ointment, balm or liniment to relieve pain.

The text describes mint as hot and dry in the third degree. Small plants with dense foliage are best. Mint is suitable for those with cold and wet stomachs, while those with warm stomachs may be harmed by it. However, that can be remedied with a little vinegar and oil. Mint is basically suitable for people with a cold and wet temperament, for old folk, for use in winter and in cold climes.

Several species of mint are known, such as the corn or field mint, sometimes called lambs' tongues, that grows up to forty centimetres in height, water mint and horsemint. 'Green mint', found growing in moist locations such as riverbanks and ditches, is cultivated as a kitchen herb; it has lanceolate leaves and a strong peppermint flavour. Peppermint has a smooth, shiny, reddish stalk, stemmed leaves and purple flowers. The leaves and the stalk contain a lot of ethereal oil. Menthol, the main constituent of ethereal oil, is effective against bacteria and parasites, cools and anaesthetises the skin, and increases the blood flow where applied. Dissolved in alcohol, menthol is useful in treating hyphomycosis. In addition, peppermint has an antispasmodic effect on muscles and is used to treat colic and flatulence. Peppermint also stimulates the liver, gallbladder and bile flow. Azulenes in the ethereal oil have anti-inflammatory properties.

Having come from England, peppermint reached the continent in about 1780. In many countries it is used mainly as a tea, but also to flavour sweets, liqueurs, salads and meat dishes.

SYMBOLISM
Symbolises the nymph who was transformed into mint by Persephone.

MEDIEVAL MEDICINE
Invigorating effect after fainting; cures hiccups and nausea.

MEDICINAL EFFECT
Rich in ethereal oils, used to treat respiratory tract and digestive organs; dried, it is used mainly as a tea.

Austrian National Library, Vienna. Cod. ser. nov. 2644, sheet 34r

· Denta ·

aDenta 2plo. ca. 7 fic. i. ʒ. Eceto pua minuta fpiffoz folioz. uiuntur; foueit fto frio.7 huo.
nocumitum. nocet fto. calo · Remo nocumiti eu medico aceto 7 olo · Quid giũt fanguine
calʒ fouenuit. fris 7 huis fenibʒ. hyeme 7 fris regioibʒ.

COMMON RUE, *Ruta*

The common rue is mentioned in the famous plan of the monastery at St. Gallen (around 820) and in the *Hortulus* by Walahfrid Strabo (808/809–849). It is shown in this miniature as three shrubs with delicate branches out of which two girls, one standing, the other sitting, are weaving garlands. According to Walahfrid Strabo, the rue's root fibres banish harmful poisons.

In the Middle Ages, rue, which originates from the eastern Mediterranean, was considered to be a miracle herb. According to Dioscorides, it was useful in treating snakebites, for cats that kill chickens, for people with bad breath and a whole host of other things. It was later claimed to be effective against the plague, 'foul air' (miasma) and nightmares. Rue turns golden when placed beside a body in its coffin. Numerous authors claimed that rue, taken in larger doses, was an abortifacient. Among the names given to it by witches was 'moly', the herb given to Odysseus to protect him against Circe's spells (cf. fig. 3, p. 10).

The renowned Dominican friar Albertus Magnus (*c.* 1193–1280) compiled a list of rue's beneficial properties: "It acts as an astringent when applied to the face and especially when its sap is mixed with that of fennel and honey and used as an eye ointment or swallowed. It also promotes digestion and stimulates the appetite and fortifies the stomach and is good for the spleen. It represses any sexual urge or desire. When eaten, it reduces fever, as does an application of its oil. It counteracts poisons."

As late as the 16th and 17th centuries, rue was still being recommended as a means to preserve chastity.

These characteristics are also reflected in the *Viennese Tacuinum* whose text recommends that rue, described as having the power to cure epileptics and those who have been poisoned, should be eaten while green and fresh. It produces fiery humours and is good for people of a cold and wet complexion, for the elderly and those with a weak constitution; it should be taken in autumn, winter, and at the beginning of spring and may be used in cold and wet regions. Rue is said to thrive best in the shadow of a fig tree.

The belief that rue can banish spirits can be traced to Aristotle's day. The renowned physician Galen of Pergamum attested that rue could "extinguish the passions of Venus".

The plant does indeed contain an ethereal oil consisting of around ten substances. In homeopathy, an extract of the fresh plant is used to strengthen vision and to treat rheumatism, neuralgia and excessive menstruation.

SYMBOLISM
As a protection against spells.

MEDIEVAL MEDICINE
Miracle herb used to cure the plague and 'foul air'; represses the libido.

MEDICINAL EFFECT
Ethereal oil containing many different substances, used in homoeopathy to treat rheumatism, neuralgia and excessive menstruation.

Austrian National Library, Vienna. Cod. ser. nov. 2644, sheet 35r

Ruta.

Ruta. complo. calẓ ẓ sicca. mᵒ. Electio uiridis recens. iuuamentum. ꝗ fert toxicatis ꝝ epilen͞
nocumentum. cōat scelam. Remotio nocumēt. cū aceto. oleo ꝝ sale. Quid gn̄at humoꝛes acu͞
tum. Conuenit. frigis ꝝ huis. sciłb; ꝝ decrepitis. hÿeme autumpno ꝝ pncipio ueris. frīs ꝝ huīs
rgiombus.

ROSES, *Roxe*

Ancient medicine recognised six parts of the rose that were beneficial to a person's health: the head of the flower and the rest of the leaf, the pollen and the stamens, the stalk and the leaf stem.

Christian symbolism accords the rose an eminent place alongside the lily (p. 40). It became especially significant in connection with the late medieval cult of the rosary. In cosmic terms, a blooming rose, the sign of Mary's motherhood, symbolises the rejuvenation of mankind and nature. Like the lily, the white rose became a symbol of virginity and the purity of the Mother of God; the red rose became both a symbol of the part Mary played in Christ's Passion and of her perfect love. In another Christian association, the rose was a symbol of the saints' bloody martyrdom that came to be applied to Christ, the king of all martyrs.

Venantius Fortunatus (second half of the 6th century), Basil the Great (around 330–379) and Ambrosius (around 340–397) associated roses with paradise. Especially in the late Middle Ages, the Madonna was frequently portrayed in a bower ('Madonna in a Rose Garden'). This genre of painting depicting the garden of Paradise surrounded by roses is a modification of the theme found in courtly society. The latter forms the basis of the portrayal in the Viennese *Tacuinum sanitatis*: in the right-hand half of the picture, a lady and a gentleman in wide, flowing robes are shown picking red and white blossoms from a rose bush and presenting them to another garlanded lady dressed in bright red who places the roses in her lap. As in other miniatures in the manuscript, the vegetation around the bush is sparse and a row of bulbous plants lines the foreground.

According to the description in the *Viennese Tacuinum*, the rose has a cold complexion in the first degree and a dry in the third, while others say in the second degree. Preference should be given to fresh roses from Suri and Persia. Their beneficial effect is especially felt through the warmth generated in the head, but this can cause the sense of smell to be impaired. Some claim camphor balances out this problem while others recommend the crocus. Roses produce no fruit and are suitable for people of a warm complexion, for adolescents, for warm seasons of the year and in hot parts of the world.

SYMBOLISM
Symbol of Mary's motherhood, symbol of paradise, the martyrdom of Christ and the saints

MEDIEVAL MEDICINE
Rose extracts were used in ointments, perfume, syrups and sugar.

Roxe ꝓlo.fri. inp.sic.m̄z. al'iz. Etectō rees de iun̄ ꝑsia sumani. cerebro ea. noeumet
efficit quibzdā guedie; ꞇ strecturā ol'fut. Remō noeti cū cāphora. al'eteo. Qd' gn̄at.oꝑ2
ueit eā. iuuenibz. ea t̄ribz ꞇ eā regloibz.

LILIES, *Lilia*

The miniature with the lily portrays a woman kneeling on the left and a man standing on the right. Both are cutting flowers and placing them in a two-handled vase. As elsewhere in the Viennese manuscript, the couple are strikingly shown in profile. The ground covering of grass is symbolised by the bulbous plants in the foreground, while the background is painted in neutral, parchment-like colours.

In Solomon's *Song of Songs*, the beauty of the lily is compared with the physical charms of the bride and groom. The white lily (*Lilium candidum L.*) became a symbol of purity and unblemished beauty and was seen both as a divine symbol of light and as an aristocratic attribute. In symbolic terms, it usually refers to Mary and Christ. In some depictions of the Annunciation, lilies are depicted in a vase beside the Virgin Mary. The flowers represent the role of the Mother of God as a vessel in which the seed of God is brought into full bloom. The lilies thus refer both to Mary's purity and to Christ's glory.

Because of its brilliant white flowers, the lily was a popular motif in Jewish and Christian art. Since the Gothic age it became ever more prevalent as a symbol of purity. This is especially true of the white lily. The brilliant white of the lily's flowers symbolises chastity and virginity. Together with the rose, whose red represents Mary's role in Christ's Passion, the lily can be said to be the main floral symbol of the Virgin Mary. According to the *Book of Nature* (1348/1350), an important work by Konrad of Megenberg (*d.* 1374), lilies have the power to drive away snakes and thus also to dispel evil.

According to the *Viennese Tacuinum* the lily has a hot complexion in the second degree and a dry one in the third degree. Preference should be given to sky-blue lilies. Lilies are an antidote to a 'bursting brain', but are harmful in that they can also cause headaches because of their coldness. Camphor can alleviate this problem, however. Strained nerves can be effectively soothed using an ointment made from the lily. Ground in a mortar and mixed with well-hung bacon, it is said to cure corns on the toes after three days of application. Lilies do not bear fruit, are suitable for people of a cold complexion, for the elderly and for women, and for use in winter and northern climes.

SYMBOLISM
Indicative of Mary's purity and the glory of Christ.

MEDIEVAL MEDICINE
Wards off snakes and used as an antidote to a 'bursting brain'.

MEDICINAL EFFECT
The white lily is used to cure swelling and burns.

Lilia.

Lilia. ɔplō. ca. in 2°. sic in 3°. Electio celestia. iuuamn̄. Resoluunt sup̄fluitatē cerebri. ⁊ purgant aq̄ cituam. nocumn̄. nocent sodē exfit. Remō noc̄ti cū camphora. Quō gn̄ant. ofō ueniunt. frī. senib3 ⁊ mulierib3. hyeme ⁊ septētrioālib3.

VIOLETS, *Viole*

Two figures in red robes are shown collecting the violet's dark blue flowers that are so small they can barely be seen among the dark and light-green leaves encircling them. The only vertical axis in the composition is provided by a tree that soars up into the sky, thereby breaking the monochrome background of the vellum.

The violet was known even in antiquity. The renowned physician Hippocrates recommended its use for the expulsion of a stillbirth, while Dioscorides used it to calm his stomach. It was considered the best antidote for a hangover and, during the Middle Ages, was highly thought of as being beneficial for headaches. Folk medicine made frequent use of the violet as a cure for coughs, bronchitis and as a poultice for skin ailments. Farmers used the flower as an oracle to tell them when to start gathering in the harvest.

The violet has appeared in medieval panels as a symbol of the Virgin Mary since the early 15th century, prompted by the *Song of Songs* (2, 12) whose *Flos campi* was equated with the violet. A combination of the rose, lily and violet, flowers associated with the Virgin Mary often referred to as the *Rosa claritatis*, *Lilium castitatis* and the *Viola humilitatis*, allude to the virtues of clarity, chastity and humility. Mary's humility is often suggested in paintings by the use of violet-blue for her cape.

The violet has a cold complexion in the first degree and a wet one in the second. Preference should be given to lapis-lazuli-coloured violets with abundant leaves which, in cooking, should be brought briefly to the boil. The brew then yields a vinegar that helps to lower a high temperature. The main benefit of fragrant-smelling violets is that they cleanse the gall bladder when an infusion is taken. The fragrance of the violet can calm a flaming temper. Like roses and lilies, violets have no side-effects, and can be particularly beneficial for adolescents and for those with a warm and dry complexion. The effect is best in the summer and in southern climes.

The flower, especially its root, actually contains various laxative and purgative substances. The pansy, *Viola tricolor*, is nowadays used to treat children's rashes, diarrhoea, fits of coughing and infections of the urinary tract.

Moreover, the violet may be used to increase diuretic and diaphoretic functions.

SYMBOLISM
The Virgin Mary; a symbol of humility.

MEDIEVAL MEDICINE
Cure for hangovers, coughs, stomach and headaches.

MEDICINAL EFFECT
Cleansing and slightly laxative properties.

*Austrian
National Library, Vienna.
Cod. ser. nov. 2644, sheet 39r*

Vitole.

Vitole. coplo. fri. in p̃. hii. in ž. Electio lazule. multiplitium foliorũ. uiuauitu: colozate.
av fienesim bibite. purgant coleram. n occunitum. carno ex fri noce̅t. Quid gũant. o.
huenunt. cal. ʒ. sic. unienibʒ. estate ʒ mioioalibʒ.

MANDRAKE, *Fructus mandragore*

The mandrake (*Mandragora officinalis L.*), a mandragora nightshade, with a human-shaped root, is among the most enigmatic of plants. Although it is mentioned in almost all medical manuscripts, it was to be found nowhere in central Europe.

This miniature in the Viennese manuscript shows how a root collector on the right-hand side of the picture is turning to flee. On the left, a plant with a human-shaped root and large, arrow-like leaves can be seen having been pulled slightly out of the ground; it is tied to a black-and-white dog that is drinking from a bowl of water in the foreground. In the Middle Ages the mandrake was considered to be half man and half herb.

Josephus Flavius (37–93 AD) in his 'Jewish War' and, later, the herbal of Pseudo-Apuleius tell the story of a plant, seemingly the mandragora, whose root tries to escape from the person pulling it up. Anyone who uprooted one was said to die. According to the texts, the magical mandragora root screams deafeningly when it is pulled out of the ground and that it is better extracted by a dog that then dies

instead of the person. Because the mandragora root was said to cry like a new-born child, it was given to women to ease period and labour pains and as an abortifacient.

It is uncertain whether the mandragora was a magic potion or a pharmacologically useful drug in the modern meaning of the phrase. On the one hand, it is known that the round fruit of the *Mandragora officinalis* contains the alkaloids L-hyoscyamine and scopolamine and has an anaesthetising effect, which gave rise to its use in operations and difficult births. The Swiss botanist and anatomist Gaspard Bauhin (1560–1624) recommended that the mandrake should be applied only externally, for instance in cases of excessive menstruation or madness. On the other hand, the view of the strangely shaped and forked rhizome as a talisman clearly indicates its place in popular superstition that encompassed all social classes. It was widely believed that the mandrake could also cause eclipses of the sun and the moon.

According to the herbal of Pseudo-Apuleius, the mandrake, known today to be poisonous,

was regarded as an antidote to eye infections, lentigo, snakebites and aching joints. In the Middle Ages, the plant was described by various authors including Hildegard of Bingen (1098–1179), who believed that the devil's influence was more apparent in this plant than in any others and that it had the ability to encourage humans to do both good and evil. These generalisations about the plant's effects are exemplified in the *Tacuinum* miniatures in an explanation stating that everybody who inhales the fragrance of the mandragora's fruit protects themselves against severe headaches and insomnia. A poultice made from the plant is said to help prevent skin infections. The mandragora's fruit may not be edible, but it aids those of fiery temperament and adolescents in the summer and in southern climes.

SYMBOLISM
Half man, half herb, kills the man who uproots it.

MEDIEVAL MEDICINE
Used to ease period and labour pains and as an abortifacient.

MEDICINAL EFFECT
Contains L-hyoscyamine and scopolamine; has an anaesthetising effect.

Austrian National Library, Vienna. Cod. ser. nov. 2644, sheet 40r

Fructus mandragore. opto fri. mj. sic. i 2. Electo magni odoriferi urinani. odorado stu sedl.
calam. 7 uigilias. emplando elefantie 7 ifectoib; nigris cutis. nocumi. ebetat sensus. Re
noctī. cū fructu edere. Quid gnūr nō e comestibile prueniet. ca. uuerib; estate 7 mdiamis.

In western art, spring is personified by Flora, the Roman goddess of flowering plants. According to Ibn Botlan, each season corresponds to one of the four elements that make up the universe. Spring stands for air, and because air is said to be between fire and water, spring unites heat and moisture.

This spring miniature shows courtly lovers wearing robes and shoes of delicate red and blue shades sitting in front of a hedge of red and white roses and two trees full of birds. In formal terms, this miniature surpasses many others in the Viennese manuscript because all the figures form a unity, and their varied and elegant movements are superior to the profile drawings of faces found elsewhere. The articulation of the hands of the two figures on the left indicate that the picture's theme is one associated with this time of year, that of love.

In the literature of late antiquity and the Middle Ages, the motif of the *locus amoenus*, the 'pleasant place', is frequently associated with other natural subjects such as the garden, eternal spring and paradise. This image takes much of its inspiration from Virgil's *Eclogues* and from the *Song of Songs* in the Old Testament (4, 12–16). The latter's myth of Creation culminates in a garden and Christians, too, like to envisage the home of the Blessed as a garden. Hrabanus Maurus (*d.* 856) described spring as new life gained through baptism or the resurrection of the flesh.

Spring is usually warm and moderately wet in the second degree. A happy medium is preferable. Generally described as good for animals and for everything growing in the earth, spring is harmful for wet bodies because it causes rot, but damage may be prevented through cleaning. Finally, the text describes spring as good for people of a cold, dry and temperate complexion, for adolescents and others in almost all regions.

SYMBOLISM

Flora, the Roman goddess of flowering plants, personifies spring. Spring is also associated with the image of paradise as a garden.

MEDIEVAL MEDICINE

Good for people of cold, dry and temperate complexions.

Austrian National Library, Vienna. Cod. ser. nov. 2644, sheet 55v

Ver.

Ver. ꝯplo. ca. tꝑate. hui. mꝰ. Aeꝛ medui. el. uuuam. ꝯ feꝛt uꝉr aialib; ꞇ tiꝛ naſcētib; noꝺu.
noꝺet coꝛb; ulhumidis. qꝛ faeit i eis putreduṅe. Remȯ noꝺti mundifieando coꝛ. Geꞇiatuꝛ
i co humoꝛ bonus ꞇ ſanguis multus. ꝑuenit ſtꝛ a. ſiꝭꝰ ꞇ tꝑatis uuuenib; ꞇ Alꝭs tꝑatis regio
nib; ꞇ fere omnib;.

Summer, *Estas*

As in the miniatures portraying the other seasons (pp. 46, 50, 52), 'Summer' also depicts agricultural activity typical of the time of year, in this case the wheat harvest.

In the foreground, a few wisps of grass contrast with the light-coloured soil while in the centre and background, the light hues of the wheat field stand out against the darkness of the earth. On the right-hand side, a man and a woman are busy gathering in the wheat; two sheafs of harvested wheat have been placed in front of a tree in the middle of the picture. On the left-hand side, a man wearing a garland of wheat and holding small bundles of the cereal in his hands faces the observer directly; another garland is even tied around his waist. The contrast between this man's frontal pose and the profile view of the two other figures harvesting the crop is a formal characteristic of many miniatures in the Viennese manuscript.

Each season is usually associated with a Biblical event. While autumn is associated with the grape harvest (p. 50), following on from the parable about the labourers in the vineyard (Matthew, 1–16), Ruth's gleaning in the cornfields (Ruth 2, 2f.) stands for summer; and Christ's resurrection ('Christ as the gardener', Mark 16, 9; John, 14–18) symbolises spring (p. 46). The theoretic background to these associations is based on the notion of all natural phenomena being incorporated in the cosmos of Christian salvational history. In connection with the four elements, summer is associated with fire.

The first part of summer – when the sun is in the house of Cancer – is considered to be the healthiest time for the body. It dries up excessive fluid that food causes to accumulate and heals illnesses brought on by cold winter. It encourages the generation of digestive fluids as well as other dry substances which slow the digestion.

Symbolism
Ruth gleaning corn symbolises summer which is also associated with fire.

Medieval Medicine
Dries excessive bodily fluid, heals illnesses brought on by the cold of winter.

Austrian National Library, Vienna. Cod. ser. nov. 2644, sheet 54r

Estas.

Estas. ꝙplo. ca. iñ. ꞇ sic ińl. Æctio i̇pi ꝑcipuum. meli̇ e coꝛpoꝛibꝫ. iuuani̇. diſolut ſuꝑ
fluitates. ꞇ egritudie̅s fit nocumi̇. minuit digo̅nes. ꞇ auget. colam. Remi̇ noeti cu̅ regi̇
mi̅e i̅ ſtitate. huio. Quid auget humoꝛes colicos. ꞇ ſic ꝗuenit. fi̅t. ꞇbu ſcibꝫ. ꞇ ſeptētóalibꝫ.

AUTUMN, *Autumpnus*

The grape harvest is portrayed here as an activity characteristic of autumn. No particular plant or fruit is the centre of attention; instead the focus is on the harvesting of grapes and the time of the year when this is done. The sun in the house of Libra announces the start of autumn, the time of year associated with the earth. The Latin name *autumpnus* is cognate with *autere* (to cool).

On the left, a man is shown treading grapes, while a girl hands him a basket full of the fruit. On the right, with his back to the girl, is another man who is busy picking grapes. As in the other miniatures in the manuscript, the figures are strikingly shown in profile. The elegant, even delicate, movements of these figures belie the physical effort demanded by their work. This harmonious image is mirrored in the round forms of the trees and the gentle sweep of a large vine across the picture.

The picture is thus composed of figures and countryside motifs that reveal a harmony between man and nature. Wine growing and harvesting are mentioned in the literature of all cultures, the first being the account of the Sumerian Flood. The vivid language of the Old Testament is also rich in the symbols of viniculture, but the New Testament, too, accords wine a special place in that Christians are compared with the labourers in the vineyard (Matthew, 1–16) and the violent vine-growers (Matthew 21, 34), and the Last Judgement with the grape harvest (Revelations 14, 15). The culmination of such imagery is represented by Christ's comparison of himself with the vine (John 15, 1–5).

Hildegard of Bingen (1098–1179) calls wine the 'earth's blood'. Like blood, it works in the body like a 'quickly-turning wheel' and drives the circulation of man's fluids. Moreover, she describes wine as a medicinal draught full of *virtutes*, full of *viriditas*, a refreshing breath of fresh air: 'For wine heals and pleases man with its health-giving warmth and its great strength.' According to St. Augustine, too, wine fortifies a weak stomach, refreshes tired spirits, heals the wounds of body and soul, dispels sorrow and tiredness of the soul. The Viennese *Tacuinum sanitatis* describes autumn as moderately cold in the second degree. The best part of this season is mid-autumn; it is favourable when the weather changes gradually without dramatic changes. Autumn produces melancholic juices and harms people with a 'moderate constitution' and those who are prone to consumption which is counteracted by the application of moistened cloth and the taking of baths. Autumn is a beneficial time for people of a hot and wet temperament, for adolescents, and in hot and wet climes.

Autipnus.

Autumpn. ꝯpꝉo. ſꝶ. tp̄ate m̄. Etecto meduſ ipſ. uinam. q̄datum. ꝑꝯbz ad ꝛꝛ̄ia. ut ad calidū
⁊ hū. noceꞇ. noceꞇ tp̄atis ꝯp̄ſomb̄z ⁊ diſpoⁿ⁊ ad ptꝛꝰſꝶz. Remō noꞇꞇ cū huꞇꞇtantib̄z ⁊ balneo. Od
augꞇꞇ huo̅ꞇes melecolicoꝛꝰ⁊uciꞇ. ca ⁊ hū. uiunt̄b̄z ſiue adoleſeꞇꞇtib̄z. ca ⁊ hū. regionib̄z al͛ tp̄atis.

WINTER, *Hyemps*

In keeping with the cold time of year, the winter scene is an indoor one. As was customary in late 13th and 14th-century painting, an exterior view is shown of a house with its front wall removed to reveal life inside, thereby creating the effect of a stage. Above the moulding there is a shallow upper storey with four identical pairs of windows.

An old man dressed in red is stoking the fire while a young woman unselfconsciously hitches up her skirt to warm her legs. The sight prompts a smile from the young man carrying wood into the room on his shoulders. In his left hand he carries a duck he has shot. This is possibly a reference to water that is usually associated with depictions of winter.

A man warming himself at the fire is a common motif in portrayals of winter; the woman and the young man are, however, innovative additions.

The text relates how winter is good for easing diseases of the gall bladder, in other words for 'hot' diseases, and that it fortifies the digestion. Its cold and wet nature is harmful, however, because of the increased sluggishness it induces. A good fire and warm clothes are needed to ward it off. It is no coincidence that the phlegmatic type is often portrayed as an old man sitting in a chair, his tired limbs craving warmth. Winter is good for people with a 'hot and dry' complexion, for adolescents and for people living in southern and maritime climes.

SYMBOLISM
Warming oneself at the fire is a vivid symbol of winter.

MEDIEVAL MEDICINE
Alleviates 'hot' diseases such as problems affecting the gall bladder.

Austrian
National Library, Vienna.
Cod. ser. nov. 2644, sheet 55r.

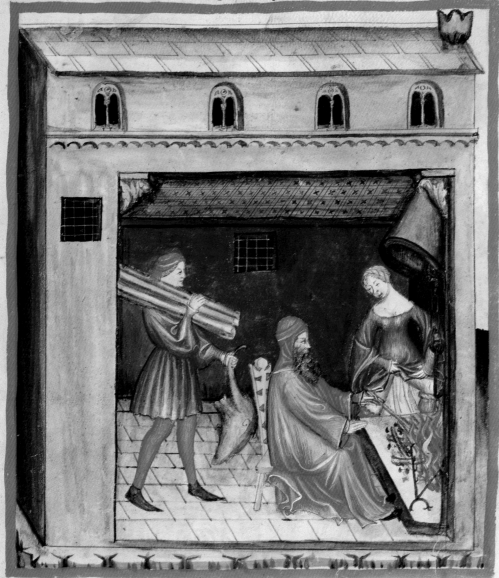

Hyemps·

hyemps· ꝯplo̅· fri· m̅a̅· hu̅· m̅a̅· �̅t se h̅ris. Electo finis eꝰ· uiuennium egritudinib; oleis et ꝯfortat dignones· noeum; nocet egritudinib; flaticis ⁊ augret flā. Remō noeti cū igne ⁊ uestimitis ꝯuenit· eaꝶ· sic⁵ iuuenib; m̅idianis ⁊ maximis regio̅mb;·

HARE MEAT, *Carnes leporine*

This miniature is one of the show-pieces among depictions of nature in the Viennese manuscript. The very high perspective gives the impression that the countryside is being viewed from a tower, with the horizon pressing hard against the picture's upper edge. In the background, the animals running around between the intricately painted leaves appear larger than life. This allows the miniaturist to include many figures, animals and plants within the picture's small area. A kaleidoscopic panorama of hunting and nature is thus presented to the viewer. Several hounds are chasing the hares, one of which appears to glance back in fear. Two beaters in colourful clothes are seen chat-

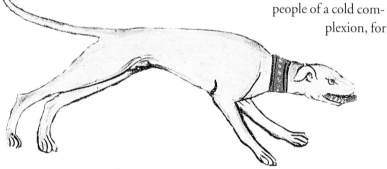

ting; one of them has a dead hare slung across his shoulders and the other has a hunting horn around his neck. Theological writing interprets the hare as an allegory of the weak and timid person who is hunted and who seeks refuge from his pursuers among the rocks, i.e. in the Church.

Hare meat is described in the text as hot and dry in the second degree and useful against putting on weight, but it can also cause insomnia. As the hare is an alert beast that sleeps with its eyes open, it could also be interpreted that this quality is transferable to those who eat its meat. The use of aromatic and complementary herbs can counteract sleeplessness in humans, however. The prohibition in the Old Testament (Leviticus 11, 6; Deuteronomy 14, 7) on eating hare meat was justified later on in history on account of the hare's fertility and promiscuity.

According to the Viennese manuscript, hare meat produces melancholic humours. Being 'hot and dry', it is described as good for people of a cold complexion, for

weak people mainly in winter and in northern climes. It is recommended that young beasts caught by hunting dogs should be eaten. Hare meat is best left to hang in the cool of the night. Leverets, cooked in water and wine with herbs, roasted with sage and cloves or baked in a pie, are very tender and agreeable to the stomach.

SYMBOLISM
The hare represents the fearful person who seeks refuge in the Christian faith.

MEDIEVAL MEDICINE
Hare meat produces melancholic humours and is good for the stomach.

*Austrian
National Library, Vienna.
Cod. ser. nov. 2644, sheet 72r*

Canes leporie. ꝯplo. ca. ꞇ. ſic m̄. Electō Juniores cāptī. pueꝛatoꝛes canes ꝟ̄uā. ꝯſeꝛūt ſupā-
tis amulta pīguedie. Aꝺꝯumtmm̄ vigilꝺur fatuit. Remō noꝛūmit eū aīꝺꝺꝺma aꝛoꝺꝺꝺ bꝫ ſb̄-
tilꝺatꝺuus. Quoꝺ gn̄ant humoꝛe meletꝯoliꝯu. ꝯueꝺunt mag. fꝛis ꝺꞇeꝛeptis. bꝛeme ꞇ fꝛis w-
gꝺomꝫ

Beef and Camel Meat, *Carnes vachine et camelorum*

This miniature belongs thematically to a sizeable number of others in the Viennese manuscript describing in detail different types of meat (gazelle, hare, mutton, goat, veal, pork, brain, dried and roasted meat [sheets 71v–75v]). These miniatures focus on the different human skills needed to obtain and enjoy meat, for instance hunting, slaughtering, cleaning, preparing or preserving. Each type of meat is shown in a way that throws some light on trade and commerce in the late Middle Ages in Italy.

The text was written by Ibn Botlan, a resident of the Middle East, (p. 24) and discusses the advantages of camel meat. The miniaturist had no choice, of course, but to show the exotic animal on the left being led into an Italian butcher's shop which, due to the rather stage-like arrangement, reminds one of the little shops frequently found tucked under an arcade. In the background, a slaughtered camel is being skinned while the animal on the chopping board is being carved up. Three customers or people interested to see what is going on are seen approaching from the right.

In allegorical terms, the way the camel goes down on its knees so that the things it is to carry can be packed onto its back, is a symbol of Christ's obedience and his arrival on earth.

According to the text, beef and camel meat is hot and dry in the second degree. Preference should be given to the meat of young, working animals. This is why it is described as beneficial for labourers and those suffering from bilious or hepatic flux. Like hare meat, beef and camel meat can also produce melancholic humours, but they can be cured with sugar and pepper. They are especially wholesome for people of a hot complexion and adolescents in the winter and in northern climes.

Symbolism
The kneeling camel is a symbol of Christ accepting his burden (i.e. his self-sacrifice).

Medieval Medicine
Good for labourers and people suffering from bilious or hepatic flux.

Austrian
National Library, Vienna.
Cod. ser. nov. 2644, sheet 74r

Carnes uachine 7 cameloru.

Carnes uacele 7 camello:um. ꝯplo. ca. 7 fic. in̄. Electo uuenum ecectitat. uuam. ꝑ̄ftant
eceitantib; fe. 7 patientib; ftuxum colicum. f̄ ꝺeumtum fatuit egtuidinib; melācolleis. Rem.
nocumti. cum. ꝫꝫ. 7 piꝑē. Qꝺ gū̄ant fanguinē gꝛoffum melēcolici. Conueiunt maḡ eꝪ
uuentib; yemē 7 feptentrionalibꝫ.

SPLEEN, *Splenes*

This image is one of a series of miniatures in the manuscript portraying and describing animals' entrails. The miniature shows the inside of a late medieval kitchen with an open fire, chimney and a pot attached to a chain, an iron stand for a roasting spit and a wall cupboard for kitchen utensils. A young boy is turning the spit and, in his left hand, he is holding a raw spleen. The cook, clad in red, is seen cleaning fresh spleens behind a table on the left.

The rich detail is typical of most of the miniatures in the Viennese manuscript and is characteristic of many interiors in the visual art of the 15th century. The great variety of everyday activities, however, contrasts with the plain and conventional exterior of the house with its shallow upper storey and four plain, arched windows.

The Latin term *splenes* is retained in the English word spleen meaning both the anatomical spleen and a bad temper. The text agrees with the interpretation that the spleen produces melancholy humours. The spleen is described as hot and dry in the second or first degree. The best spleen comes from young and fat animals, mainly pigs. It fortifies the constitution and the effects of bodily fluids. It is described as unfavourable for melancholic types, but any problem is alleviated by steaming it in fat or lots of oil. The spleen is thought to be good for people of a hot and wet complexion (sanguine types), for adolescents and those living in mountainous regions, and should be eaten mainly in winter.

SYMBOLISM
The spleen is the seat of bad temper and melancholy.

MEDIEVAL MEDICINE
Produces melancholic humours; recommended for sanguine types.

Austrian National Library, Vienna. Cod. ser. nov. 2644, sheet 80v

· Splenes ·

Splenes. ꝯplo. ca. ꝝsic. in ꝛ. aꝝ. ꝑ. Electo ex pinguib; alib; ⁊ iuuenib; ꝓpue porcorum.
uuamtum adigrossandum ꝯplone; ⁊ huores. nocumtum patientib; melencolia. Remo
nocumti cum pinguedie ⁊ oleo misto. Q̃uo gnant huores; malum ⁊ melencolic ꝗuenuit
mag calis; ⁊ huis. iuuenib; hyeme ⁊ montinis.

LAMPREYS, *Lamprete*

This miniature depicting the lamprey is among the most interesting illustrations in the whole manuscript. It is found in the section on fish (sheets 82r–84v: fresh fish, salted fish, crabs, pickled fish and ambergris). The old Latin name *Lampetra* describes the habit the fish has of attaching itself to stones using its sucker mouth.

While the manuscript contains mostly interior views, this painting shows an open-air scene of fishermen catching lampreys with their nets. One fisherman, his jerkin hitched up, is standing in a fast-flowing river trying to heave the fish out of it with both arms. The catch can be seen above him in a wooden barrel. A customer who wants to take home live fish in a white jug is seen standing on the right.

As in many other miniatures in the Viennese manuscript, the act of catching and selling are shown together. The miniaturist juxtaposes the various elements of the action by placing the image of the land above the river scene. What would normally be depicted as being in the background is shown without perspective 'above' the fisherman. The groups of trees frame the image at the sides. The only blue is that of the river whose spray and foam are depicted using white streaks.

The author says that lampreys are cold and wet in the second degree, but that they are not as wet as eels. He recommends that the fish should be taken from a river that flows across pebbles. The fish are a good source of food, but because they are unsuitable for a weak and wet stomach, they should be seasoned with salt and pepper. They taste very good when pickled in malmsey wine or when their mouths are stuffed with nutmeg and they are spiked with cloves. Lampreys are recommended for people of a warm and dry complexion (choleric types) because they produce phlegmatic humours and for adolescents in the autumn and summer and in northern areas where they can be better digested.

SYMBOLISM
Fish as a symbol of Christ.

MEDIEVAL MEDICINE
Fish are a good source of nourishment but are unsuitable for a weak stomach.

MEDICINAL EFFECT
Rich in vitamins, protein and iodine.

Austrian National Library, Vienna. Cod. ser. nov. 2644, sheet 84r

Lampte cpło fri.7 hi. iž. mioris tñ hi. q̃ anguile. Electo sluis drarctis sup petras. unia.
ĩ pinguiat 7 multũ nutriunt. Nocuistũ sto debili 7 huo; Remo noaumiti ei salintg
7 pipe. Quid gñant humoze slegmaticũ 2 ueniunt mag. ca.7 sic. iuueib; autip̃no 7 estate
septentrioalib; quia meli digezunt:

SPRING WATER, *Aqua funtium*

This miniature depicting spring water is one of numerous images in the Viennese *Tacuinum sanitatis* that consider different types of water (salt water, warm water, rain water and aluminous water). Each type has its own characteristic illustration that is more concerned with depicting daily life that showing the curative effects of a particular type of water.

Against a backdrop of jagged rocks, a basin can be seen supported on four columns. Behind the rectangular basin there is a double-arched structure with a hipped roof. A young lady, gathering her dress up in her right hand and holding the wooden bucket of water on her head in her left hand, is about to disappear through an imposing archway into a house with fantastically designed mouldings. The artist obviously wants to connect life indoors with life outside through movement. Young women carrying water in a vessel on their heads is a motif frequently found in 15th-century Italian painting and, here, it fulfils the miniaturist's wish for a realistic portrayal of nature.

Spring water is described as cold and wet in the fourth degree besides being a useful cure for inflammation of the liver and good for digestion. Cooled spring water is harmful in that it causes flatulence. A bath and mild physical exercise can provide relief. Spring water is especially wholesome for people of hot and dry complexions and for adolescents in the summer and in warm parts of the world.

SYMBOLISM
Source of eternal life, symbol of the Virgin Mary.

MEDIEVAL MEDICINE
Good for the digestion and liver problems.

MEDICINAL EFFECT
Numerous uses as mineral water.

*Austrian
National Library, Vienna.
Cod. ser. nov. 2644, sheet 88v*

Aqua fontium.

Aqua fontium. ꝯplo. frī. ꝉ bu. i. q. Electō ex fontibꝫ oriētalibꝫ. uiuani. ꝯ fert epati calo
ꝛ bigdm. Nocui. � ꝛ fatuit inflatices buias. Remo nocti cū balneo ꝛ excitio moꝛe
rato. Quid gnāt multiplicat urinam ꝯuenit mag. caꝉꝛ sic. iuuenibꝫ estate ꝛ. ca. regioibꝫ.

Snow and Ice, *Nix et glacies*

This miniature is a fantasy landscape of bizarrely shaped formations of ice and snow executed in bold strokes. The rocks open up in the centre to form a basin covered in ice.

In the foreground, a pack-donkey carrying wood on a primitive frame is making its way down into the valley, its owner prodding it in the hindquarters.

The miniaturist here succeeds in his attempt not simply to list the four elements, but to incorporate them in comprehensive genre scenes. The fantastic character of this landscape, with its non-naturalistic and symmetrical cliff formations, clearly shows that the character of the miniatures in the Viennese *Tacuinum sanitatis* is determined both by the close observation of nature and artistic licence.

The text informs the reader that snow and ice are cold and wet in the third degree. Both have beneficial effects when made from good fresh water. Snow and ice stimulate the digestion, but make one cough; to avoid this, a moderate amount should be drunk before enjoying snow and ice.

Moreover, snow and ice cause painful joints and paralysis, but are good for people of a hot complexion and for adolescents, mainly in summer and in southern climes.

Symbolism
Legends surrounding the Virgin Mary.

Medieval Medicine
Stimulates the digestion, but also causes painful joints and paralysis.

Medicinal Effect
Relieves bruises and swelling.

*Austrian
National Library, Vienna.
Cod. ser. nov. 2644, sheet 90r*

Nix ꞁ glaties.

Nix ꞁ glaties. Complo. fri. ꞁ hu. in̄z. Electo eraqua dulci ꞁ bona. uuanī. meliorat digo-
nem. ꞁ oeunitum tussim ꞁoueꞇ. Remo̅ noeti bitedo antea moẟei. Quo g̅ n̅at uesica-
tione; inetinatuꞁ; ꞁ palissm̄ Conuelt mag. ca̅. uuisinb; estate meridianis regioib;.

The Interlocutor, *Confabulator*

This miniature is found in the Viennese codex between the representation of sleep and one about talking in one's sleep. Its position is further supported in the text when it is says that dialogue is one of the main causes of sleep. There is, therefore, a logic in the sequence of these miniatures that at first sight do not appear to belong together.

The old man dressed in red at the left of the picture, vaguely reminiscent of the one in Winter (p. 52), is described as a *Confabulator*, an interlocutor. An old woman with a white headscarf sits opposite him; she holds a spindle in her left hand. In the foreground, a young man dressed in red and two children are gathered round the fire to listen to the old man's stories. With his left hand, the old man is gesticulating and in his right hand he holds a staff. This scene takes place inside; a door with a round arch separates it from an adjacent room and consoles with a decoration of leaves supported on two column-like structures separate it from the foreground, thus creating the impression of a stage.

The author says in his description of the miniature that it is good when the interlocutor's personality appeals to the person wanting to sleep because when someone is enjoying a story, it not only improves his senses and spirits, but also his digestion. It is harmful, though, when several people talk at the same time and one wants to listen only to one of them. For obvious reasons, the person one does not want to listen to should be asked to remain silent. Conversation is described as good for everybody except for children, at every time of the year but mainly in winter and in populated areas.

Medieval Medicine
Deep sleep follows good conversation.

Austrian National Library, Vienna. Cod. ser. nov. 2644, sheet 100v

. Confabulator .

Confabulato̅ .iii. c̅ .ima c̅x̅ sompu. Electo ꝛ uciens n̅e uolc̅tis doꝛmir. uiuam. delectatib; ipa̅.
meliorat i ei uigones ꝛ sens̅ ꝛ s̅p̅b. Slocuintium audi̅r ples ꝛ fabulatoꝛes. cu uoluit n̅ uni audic.
Remo̅ noc̅ti i po̅ne̅r scilentiu̅. illi /q̅ audir no̅ cu̅p. Comicit oib; ꝯplonib; oib; etatib;. pt̅er
pu̅is. oi t̅p̅: s̅ mag breme ꝛ regioi hi̅tate.

Horse Riding, *Equitatio*

A few miniatures in the last section of the manuscript depict genre scenes that, strictly speaking, are no longer concerned with particular plants or medicines, but which focus rather on different aspects of daily living. The Interlocutor (p. 66) is not the only such image; others describe sports such as fencing, or day-to-day subjects like sleep, awakening, going for a walk, singing, making music, being happy, drunk or even sick!

The miniature portraying an equestrian scene can be described as one of the best quality images in the manuscript. A richly-clad couple is riding past a two-storey building whose upper floor has two double windows, each framing a couple. The storeys are separated by a frieze with a semicircular pattern. Along the side façade there is a projecting first-floor loggia, with each opening surmounted by small, decorative gables – the whole resting on an arcade of slender columns.

A flight of stairs leads up to the loggia; a lady with one white rose and three red roses (p. 38) stands at its head, an allusion to love and the couples in the first-floor windows.

The text describes riding as an activity that should preferably induce perspiration. Movement should not be over-strenuous, and that is why it is advantageous to ride on flat terrain with no obstacles and at temperate times of the year. The advantages of riding are numerous: the natural warmth it generates stimulates digestion; in addition, riding opens the pores and sweat cleanses. Practiced to excess, riding can also cause harm, however. Wet objects and rest are the required remedies.

MEDIEVAL MEDICINE
Opens the pores and cleanses them by sweating; stimulates digestion.

. Equitatio .

Equitatio na eſ mot' quida moderatͦ· mediante equitatͦ. Eecto pucͦis ſudoꝛ· eſ uiua fac
qꝛ eͤcitat caloꝛe: nͣlem/ ipinqᷓ agitat ad dıgoͤne: puͦcandaꝛ ꞇ ſbtiliadas ſiſtuſ Ho qꝛ apͭ pꝛ
reꝛ ꞇ meat' mundificat cͣ ſudoꝛe. Teͤtio idurat ımbꝛa coꝛ eͤcıtıo ꞇ ſıͤcatoͤ· Jocͣnituꝛ cͣ eͤcedeꝛ
i eo. Remͦ cͣ huıſ ꞇ qete ſqueͤt mag· caſ huıſ pͭcıs ꞇ uıueıͤs teͤpatıs tͦbͣs planıs regıoıbͥ
tͦatis eͤpedıtıs:

AGATE, *Lapis acatus*

The *Physiologus* describes how pearl fishers use agate to locate their quarry. Attached to a sturdy line, the agate is lowered into the sea. The pearl fishers dive into the water and follow the weighted line down to the seabed where the agate will be found having come to rest on a bed of pearl oysters.

The upper left-hand section within the wide frame is filled by the outline of a boat and two oarsmen. The man on the right is letting out a chain which the other pearl fisher holds as he is lowered head-first into the depths. The way in which the diver's naked body, the boat's ochre colouring and the oar's flat paddle seem to glow through the water is exceptional in the quality of its execution and – as is the case with other miniatures in this illuminated manuscript – suggests that the artist probably had equally good material from which to work.

In the *Physiologus*, the agate that locates the pearls symbolises John the Baptist, the man who pointed out the precious pearl of Jesus Christ and who identified him as the future Redeemer: "Look, there is the Lamb of God; it is he who takes away the sin of the world" (John, 1 29). The sea is the world, the pearl fishers symbolize the host of Old Testament prophets and Christ himself is the crowning jewel. Whoever wants to own such a precious gift is urged by the Bible to sell his possessions and give to the poor (Matthew 13, 45f. and 19, 21).

SYMBOLISM
Agate locates pearls on the seabed and symbolises John the Baptist who finds Christ.

Burgerbibliothek, Bern. Codex Bongarsianus 318, sheet 20v

DE LAPIDE ACATO

Quando artifices quaerunt margarita p̃ctm̃ inue-
munt eam in grossiorem resticulam dimittunt eam
in mare. Uenit ergo acathes sup margaretam & n̄
mouetur. Statim ergo ori naturi secuntur restem
& inuenunt margaretā. Conchos uocttur pisces qui
in marie aperit ossium & suscipit cceuram & radio
solis simul & lune. & sic concipit margaretā. Acater
ergo qui inuenit margaretā. accipitur iohannes
ostendit p̃caosā margaretā dnm ihm xp̃m de quo
dixit. Ecce agnus dī. ecce qui tollit peccta mundi.
haec ē uera margareta. quē tu homo si uolueris
habere uende bona tua & dā p̃ uperibus & inuenies eā.

LION, *Leo*

The patriarch Jacob, identified by a halo and his right hand raised in blessing, stands on the left on a ledge which forms part of a range of mountains, the slopes of which are wooded. The lion described in the text as the "young lion Judah, my son" approaches majestically from the right. The scene is framed by a high mountain range to the rear and by pairs of cattle, bears and deer to the front.

The miniature exemplifies the symbolic importance of the lion as the king of animals. This role is alluded to at the beginning of the text and in Jacob's blessing of Judah (Genesis 49, 9), "Judah, you lion's whelp". The three characteristics of the lion as applied to Christ are then explained (p. 90). The passage from Genesis has been interpreted in different ways over the centuries. The representation of Jacob's blessing in the famous altar at Klosterneuburg by Nikolaus of Verdun (1181) was said to refer to Christ's resurrection. In eastern Germany in the late Middle Ages, the image of the mother of God on a lion was developed, leading her son as the promised lion of Judah. In the Middle Ages, the three natures of the lion were expanded to include 'magnanimity' towards those who devote their lives to his name. The function of the 'king' (of all animals) was frequently associated with the role of judge and warrior fighting falsehood and lies.

SYMBOLISM
Christ as the Lion of Judah.

Burgerbibliothek, Bern. Codex Bongarsianus 318, sheet 7r

EST LEO REGALIS OM
mum animalium & bestiarum · Ideo & iacob
benedicens iuda dicebat · Catulus leonis iuda
filius meus & cetera · Physiologus narrat
de leone qui tres naturas hab&
prima natura leonis · haec est ·

EAGLE, *Aquila*

This well-preserved miniature is compositionally striking for its extensive view across a stretch of countryside that reveals no specific features. The eagle in this portrayal has its wings spread. The roughness of the terrain is indicated by broad greyish and reddish-brown brush strokes. At the top, the miniature ends in a light green band. The blue water in the foreground can be understood as a reference to the healing and rejuvenating spring water mentioned in the *Physiologus*.

The *Physiologus* describes how the eagle ages and how his wings become heavy and his sight dims. To counteract these effects, he flies near the sun, spreads his wings, burns his old feathers and comes down to a spring into which he dives three times and rises again, renewed. The Bible says: "And my youth is ever new like an eagle's" (Psalm 103, 5).

The eagle's nature is interpreted in such a way that the spiritual source, the word of God, can help "all those who discard not their ancient robes". Christ, the 'sun of righteousness' (Malachi 4, 2) removes the devil's old garments and baptises him in the name of the trinity, thereby making of the old man a new one in God's image.

SYMBOLISM
Symbol of Christ's Resurrection and Ascension, but also a symbol of the devil.

Burgerbibliothek, Bern. Codex Bongarsianus 318, sheet 10v

peccatum non fecit. & humiliauit se ut nos exaltaret.
Bene ergo physiologus narrat de nocticorace.

DE NATURA UOLATILE AQUILE

Dauid dicit renouabitur sicut aquile iuuentus
tua. Physiologus dix de aquila. qm si senuerit grava
buntur alę eius & caliginant oculi ipsius. Quid ergo facit?
quaerit fontem aqua munda & uolat in aera solis ex
tendit alas & descendit in fontem aquae. Baptizatur
per ter & ascendit reprobuit caliginem oculorum &
renouabitur & nouus fit. Sic autem & tu ueterem
indumentum habens & caliginant tibi oculi quaere spiri
tale fontem di uerbum. qui dix me dereliquerunt fontem
uiuam aquę. Et uolens in altitudinem solis iustitiae
ihs xps. Et ipse exui te ueterem indumentum diaboli
& baptizare in sempiternum fontem. In nomine pa
tris & filii & sps sci. hoc ergo dauid dicit renouabitur
sicut aquila iuuentus tua.

Many pages in the *Bern Physiologus* are devoted to images of the snake because of its role as a symbol of the Devil. Like the lion (p. 72) and the eagle (p. 74), the snake is also attributed with a number of qualities that are sometimes contradictory. The beast is both clever and cunning but it is also corrupt and evil.

The *Physiologus* describes the viper as having the face of a man down to its navel and the shape of crocodile as far as its tail. John the Baptist likens snakes to the Pharisees who killed both the Prophets and Christ (Matthew 3, 7; Luke 3, 7). The text then goes on to discuss the snake's second nature. Its eyes dim with age (cf. the eagle, p. 74). To rejuvenate itself and to loosen its skin, it fasts for forty days before squeezing through a crack in the rocks to remove its old skin. This quality of "wary serpents" (Matthew 10, 16) is described as one to be emulated by a believer striving to attain eternal life.

The snake's third nature is revealed when it goes to drink at the water's edge. When it does so, it leaves its venom in its cave. The text interprets this as a sign for the believer on his way to eternal life that he must renounce all wickedness and put it behind him.

The text incorporates a magnificent miniature depicting the snake's fourth nature. The picture shows a man killing a wriggling snake by stabbing it with his spear. The text explains that the snake exposes its body to its killer, but not its head. The allegorical meaning here is that, in times of temptation and persecution, a Christian ought to offer up his whole body except for his head as "… every man has Christ for his Head …" (1 Corinthians, 11, 3).

SYMBOLISM
The four natures of the snake: clever and cunning, corrupt and evil.

MEDICINAL EFFECT
Snake venom had diverse pharmacological uses.

Burgerbibliothek, Bern. Codex Bongarsianus 318, sheet 12v

DE QUARTA NATR SERPETS

Quando uenerit homo & uoluerit
occidere eum totum corpus tradit
capit aut custodit· Debemus & nos
intempore temptationis totum cor
pus tradere· caput aut custodire ide
xpm nonnegantes sicut fecerunt
sci martyres omnis enim caput xps est

DE NATR FORMICAE

Quando recondit triticum interra diuidit grana eius
induas partes neforte hiemis conphendit eam & infundens
pluuia & germinent grana & fame pereant· Et uuerba
ueteris testamenti adspiritalem intellectum nequan
dolittera occidit· Paulus dix qm lex spiritalis est· Sol um
enim carnaliter adtendentes iudei fame necatisunt
& homicide factisunt prophetarum

DE NATR FORMICES SECTIO

Sepius inagrou ascendit inspi
ca intempore messis & deponit gra
na eius priusquam ascendit adorat
deorsum spicam & ab odore magna

PANTHER, *Panthera*

The panther's noble stride is reminiscent of that of the lion (p. 72). Three animals (a deer, a fox and a wild boar) are leaping and bounding towards him. The venomous snake, a dangerous adversary of the panther, appears at the top of the prominent hill in the right-hand section of the picture. Lighter bands of colour on the horizon indicate daybreak.

The *Physiologus* describes the panther as a friend of all animals except the dragon. His is described as colourful and speckled in appearance; his behaviour, however, as very gentle. After eating, he sleeps in his hollow for three days; when he next stirs he goes outside and roars in a powerful voice. His voice is as sweet as spice and those who are near and far follow his call so that they can benefit from its sweetness.

In terms of Christianity, Jesus Christ, rising from the dead on the third day, filled all those far and near with the sweetness of faith. As with the symbolism surrounding the lion, the panther alludes to Christ's Resurrection. The panther's colourful appearance is related to the virtues of Christ who embodies purity, mercy, faith, virtue, magnanimity, harmony and peace. The panther provides a vivid example of how, in the *Physiologus*, an animal's every characteristic can be interpreted in Christian terms.

SYMBOLISM
Symbol of Christ's Resurrection and virtues.

Burgerbibliothek, Bern. Codex Bongarsianus 318, sheet 15r

herodi; diaboli sic art &dic uulpulli. &incanti
cif canticorum. Capitenobis uulpes exterminan
tesuineam d equa uinea dauid dixit.

DE ANIMALE QUIDICIT PANTHER

Propheta sic dicit factus sum sicut panter in domo
effrem. Phisiolocus sic testificat de panterio qntalis
é nature eius ut omnium animalium sit amicus
Inimicus aute é draconis. Uarium é enim aspectus
illius sicut tonica ioseph. diam &totus uarius est.
Tacit nimem animal &mansuetus ualde. Suut
manducauerit &sacius fuerit dormit in sua spe
lunca &teciadie exsurgit desomno &cumsurrexe
rit delocosuo &foris exierit uociferat uocem magna

SALAMANDER, *Salamandra*

The salamander miniature is not framed like most others in the manuscript, but is instead part of the text. The miniaturist has chosen to portray the salamander in a wooden washtub.

A possible explanation for the portrayal of the reptile as a hairy, horned satyr with bushy eyebrows and straggly beard, with no animal features at all, is that it was based on another image, painted at an earlier date. The ground is suggested in broad reddish and yellow diagonal brush strokes; the trees and bushes that sprout out of the ground are, however, tiny compared with the main motif.

The name 'salamander' is presumably of oriental origin and consists of the Arabic-Persian word *samandra* (poison) and the syllable *al*. Based on the notions of the authors of antiquity, the legend of the salamander's ability to withstand fire and its poisonous nature soon became widespread. It was said to be able to go through fire unscathed while poisoning everything that it touched. In the light of that ancient tale, the Middle Ages regarded the salamander as an elemental spirit and ruler of fire that it was able to extinguish itself. The interpretation associated with the salamander thus came to be applied to Christ who was said to have the ability to extinguish the fires of evil and to kindle the fire of goodness in its place.

The salamander was also associated with the Virgin Mary because the fire of original sin could do her no harm and could put out the flames of desire in others. More widely, the salamander is a symbol of redemption and purity.

According to the *Physiologus*, the salamander smothers flames on entering a fiery furnace or, on sliding into a washtub, makes the whole bathhouse go cold.

The Biblical parallel is found in the story of the three youths who remained unharmed on being thrown into the blazing furnace because Christ walked with them (Daniel 3, 19–30). The salamander's ability to extinguish fire is compared with the Just walking along the path of righteousness, abating the flames and stopping the lion's mouth.

SYMBOLISM
Christ as a ruler of fire; a symbol of redemption and purity.

& in inferiora terre psecutus est eum. Et effundens
de latere suo sanguinem & aquam & effugauit
draconem plauacrum regenerationis & diaboli
opera amputauit.

DE NATR ANIMALIS QUIDITS SALAMAN
DRA

Hic si introierit in fornacem ignis extinguitur ignis
aut in balneo si introierit totus balneus frigidus effici
tur. Ita erant corpora trium puerorum quos ignis
non lesit sed magis aduersarios retegit qui eos in for
nace xps sua uirtute roborauit

ELEPHANT, *Elifantus*

The *Physiologus* dedicates two separately illustrated chapters to the elephant, a beast that can be said to be the largest animal on land. The book's author had most certainly never seen a real elephant in his life, hence the reason why the animal's spiritual and allegorical importance is given greater expression. In Greek and Roman literature, the elephant, with its qualities of intelligence, purity, and eagerness to learn, gentleness and helpfulness, was viewed positively. Allegory in the Middle Ages and the modern era took its lead from the ancients and also viewed the animal positively, giving it a religious role. Perfectly white ivory is often compared with the purity of the Virgin Mary.

The first chapter about the elephant is called the 'Elephant and Mandrake' and includes a story about elephants' sexual behaviour. They set off to the Orient, to a place near Paradise, to feed off the mandrake tree before mating, an event interpreted as a reference to the Fall. The miniature shows the elephant moving towards the river of Paradise to reach the mandrake tree. In the foreground, a snake (cf. p. 76), the elephant's enemy, is seen wriggling on the ground. The bull elephant must protect his mate while she gives birth because the snake is lying in wait for the young elephant, ready to devour it. Gestation is about two years and the cow gives birth only once in her life to one young. When it is time for her to give birth, the cow wades into the water until it reaches her chest. The baby elephant floats in the water and is subsequently suckled for seven days. When the baby elephant can walk on its own legs, it leaves the water along with its parents.

It is noticeable how many of the details in this miniature are authentic, e.g. the elephant is painted in grey. The second chapter dedicated to the elephant on sheet 19v tells the story of twelve elephants that could no longer stand up and who were brought to their feet again by a small elephant. It was thought that elephants, because they lacked knee joints, could not get up again once they had fallen over. Aristotle contested that view but it still found its way into literature time and again. Because of this anatomical peculiarity, the elephant leans against a tree when it wants to sleep. The miniature has obviously been turned 90 degrees on its side to make more space for the illustration. In the *Physiologus*, the twelve elephants are equated with the prophets and the young elephant takes on the role of Christ the Saviour who humbles himself to raise those who have fallen by the wayside.

SYMBOLISM
Intelligence, chastity, gentleness and helpfulness.

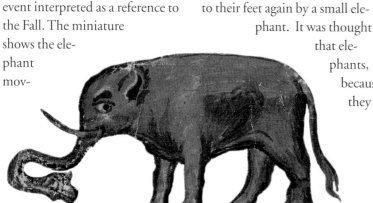

Burgerbibliothek, Bern. Codex Bongarsianus 318, sheets 19r and 19v

Mare mundus est. Nauis sca ecca inquibus ti
populi di. hic aut piscer diabolus est quir transfigu
rat se uelut inangelo lucis ut incautas animas
facilius possit decipere.

DE ELIFANTO ET MANDRACORA

Non est coitus concupiscentiae quando noluerint
facere iunctionem ambulant sup flumen para
disi &inueniunt mandracoram qui &eis femina
discurrit. Accipiens uero femina mandracora
praestat masculo &ludit cum eo donec manduc &
Et cum manducauerit masculus conuenit cum

femina & concipiet. Cum ergo tempus uene
rit ut generet intrat instagnum aquie & sic
aqua ad mamillas euir & dimittit natum. ut na
uigando sup aquas proximum habeat natem ma
tris suae. Serpens aut inimicus est aelifanto quia
pedibus suis interficit eum.

CREATION CYCLE

The miniatures in this bestiary are arranged in the order of the Creation (Genesis 1, 1–2, 25) and show God the Father, his feet planted on the Earth, separating the water under the vault from the water above it and how the ground upon which he stands sprouts fresh growth. Another miniature shows God the Father creating the sun, moon and stars as well as the creatures of the sea and air and how, on the sixth day, he gives life to the creatures of the earth.

In this miniature (sheet 6 v) the creatures of the earth are arranged in four rows of pictures and are readily identifiable: the elephant, at the top, is followed by the hare, cat and squirrel, then the lion and dog, ram, goat, cow, horse and deer. The opposite page shows the creation of Eve (sheet 7 r).

The story of the Creation, with its accompanying miniatures, forms a picture cycle in its own right that comes before the start of the text interpreting the nature of animals. Their pictures are always set in relation to the adjacent image of Christ, an arrangement that clearly shows how the bestiary is intended to be a 'spiritual manual' with a strong Christian orientation. Nature is thus shown to have no inherent value in itself;

instead it derives its worth from being part of the 'bigger picture' of the mystery of Christian Creation.

The text in a bestiary is often prefaced by a series of self-contained images showing the days of the Creation and the naming of the animals. The opaque water-colour miniatures of the Bodleian Library's Ashmole manuscript no. 1511, sheets 4r–9r, are impressive examples from the beginning of the 13th century. The Cistercians had a noticeably keen interest in the bestiary that lasted until the late 13th century.

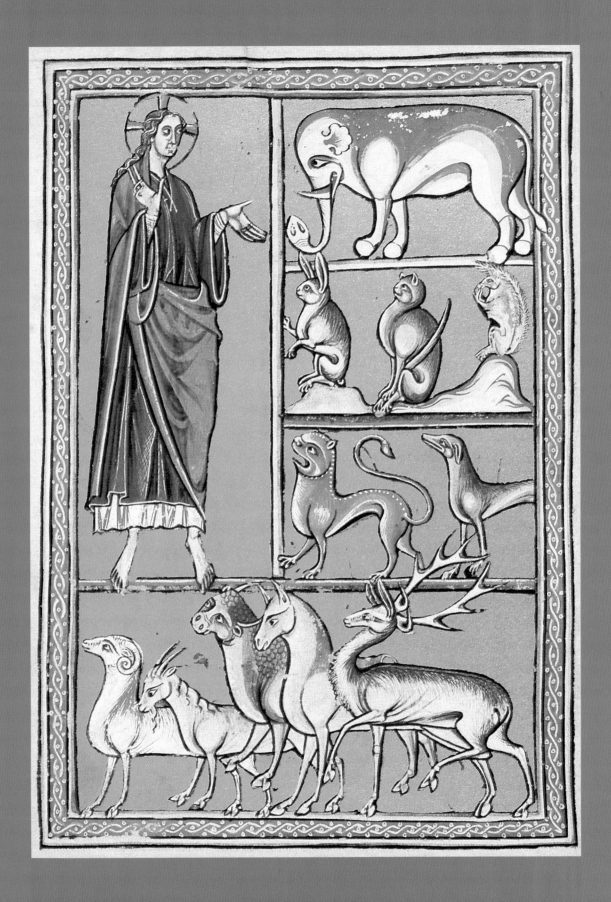

THE PEREDEXION TREE, *Peredexion*

The peredexion tree is a magic tree in India whose fruit is deliciously sweet. Doves live in the tree, build their nests in it and eat its fruit. A dragon lies in wait beneath the tree but he is unable to rest in its shadow. If a dove leaves the protection of the tree's shadow, it is killed by the dragon. The dragon flees the shadow, moving from one side of the tree to the other as the shadow crosses the ground.

The tree stands for God the Father and the tree's shadow is his son, as Gabriel announced to Mary: "the power of the Most High will overshadow you" (Luke 1, 35). The tree's heavenly fruit can be interpreted as the wisdom of the Holy Ghost that man has received in sacraments. If man holds to such wisdom, he will partake of the fruits of the spirit such as joy, peace, abstinence and patience.

Thus man is safe from the Evil One who will be thwarted in his dark deeds such as fornication, debauchery, worshipping false idols, passion, covetousness and greed. The text urges man to be like the doves, i.e. never to leave the tree of life and its shadow, in other words not to turn away from God the Father and his son. If one does, one will fall victim to the dragon, i.e. the devil.

This miniature in the Oxford Bestiary is undoubtedly one of the most ornamental in the whole manuscript. While the text mentions only one dragon, the miniature, in a convincing piece of symmetry, depicts two doves and two dragons doing battle.

SYMBOLISM

The tree as a symbol of God the Father. One should never remove oneself from the safety of the Tree of Life.

*Bodleian Library, Oxford.
Ms. Ashmole 1511, sheet 81r*

*Bodleian Library, Oxford.
Ms. Ashmole 1511, sheet 77v*

PELICAN, *Pelicanus*

The pelican is among the species of birds that no reader of bestiaries could ever have known as it lives along the banks of the Nile. The way it was reputed to live its life permitted a highly symbolic interpretation. Full of love for its children, the pelican is poorly paid in return by them. When they have grown up, they slap their parents in the face but the parents strike back and kill their young. The parents then spend three days mourning their dead children. After three days the mother pierces her own breast and lies down across them so that her blood will restore them to life.

The pelican is a symbol of Christ while Egypt stands for darkness. Just as the pelican kills its young with its beak, Christ crushes non-believers with the words of his sermons. But the pelican must weep for its dead young, just as Christ wept for the dead Lazarus. After three days the pelican uses its blood to restore life to its young, an act that early on was taken to refer to Christ's Resurrection. Thus, in the Middle Ages,the pelican became a symbol of Christ and his self-sacrifice on the Cross and was mentioned in hymns and church readers. The presence of the pelican motif on tabernacle doors and monstrances is a further indication of the symbolic link with the Eucharist.

But the pelican is also attributed with the qualities of a hermit as it only takes as much food as it needs to live. The biblical reference in this context can be found in The Book of Psalms, chapter 102, verse 6, where it is written. "I am like a pelican of the wilderness".

The complex events in the tale of the pelican are shown in the miniature in three sections of which the right-hand one is the main one showing the pelican's self-sacrifice.

SYMBOLISM
Symbol of Christ's self-sacrifice.

Bodleian Library, Oxford.
Ms. Ashmole 1511, sheet 46v

LION, *Leo*

The lion is one of the most symbolic of animals and with good reason is found at the beginning of the *Physiologus*. Just as the eagle is the king of all birds, the lion can be said to be the king of all the beasts that walk upon four legs.

According to the *Physiologus*, there are three main sides to the lion's nature. The first is that he loves to roam across the high peaks of the mountains. Using his tail, he wipes away traces of his spoor so that hunters will be unable to find him. The Christian interpretation of this says that Christ, the lion from the tribe of Judah (Genesis 49, 9; Revelations 5, 5), conceals the signs of his divinity so that he can save mankind with his incarnation.

The lion's second characteristic is that he sleeps with his eyes open. In relation to Christ, this was interpreted to mean that the son of God who dies on the Cross was buried while his divinity remained alert and sat at his Father's right hand. Psalm 121, 4 alludes to this: "The guardian of Israel never slumbers, never sleeps". The lion sleeping with his eyes open gave rise to the image of the crucified Christ.

The lion's third characteristic is that the lioness gives birth to dead young. She then watches over them for three days until her mate appears, blows into their faces and awakens them with his roar. Christ, too, was awoken from the dead on the third day.

In the literature and art of the Middle Ages, the lion is a highly contradictory being ranging from "your enemy the devil, [prowling] like a roaring lion", (1 Peter 5, 8) to the victorious lion of the Apocalypse (Revelation, 5, 5), "from the tribe of Judah, the Scion of David". Moreover, the lion is often seen as a king and judge or a symbol of imperial power.

As in the other manuscript miniatures containing a wealth of symbolism attaching to the more important animals, both pages of the *Bestiary* each have three images showing the lion's different characteristics.

SYMBOLISM
The lion's three characteristics: Christ as the Lion of Judah, Christ asleep and awake at the same time, the lion as a symbol of Christ's Resurrection.

Bodleian Library, Oxford. Ms. Ashmole 1511, sheet 10v

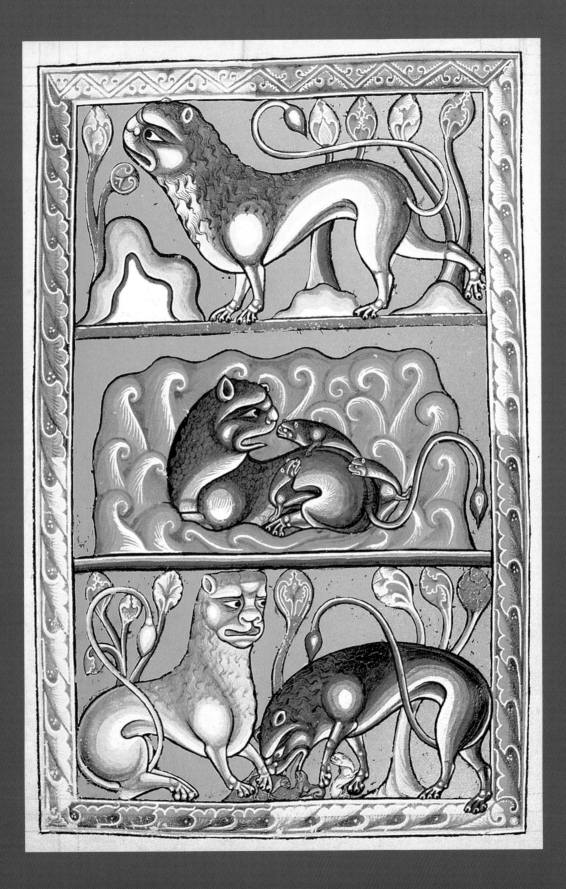

Unicorn, *Unicornis*

The unicorn is an imaginary animal from the mythology of the Middle Ages. A small animal with a straight horn in the centre of its forehead, the unicorn in the Middle Ages was typically represented as a horse or a gazelle. No hunter has the power to capture or kill one. If, however, a virgin is taken to the land of the unicorn, the beast jumps into the girl's lap and can easily be killed ('mystic unicorn hunt'). The deathblow that the unicorn receives was associated with Christ's self-sacrifice. According to the *Physiologus*, a virgin has power over the unicorn that has jumped into her lap and she can lead it to the royal palace. Konrad of Megenberg, in his *Book of Nature* (around 1348/50) stresses the connection with Christ's incarnation and underlines the attraction of chastity: "When the unicorn approaches, it abandons all its fierceness and honours the purity of the virgin's chaste body".

Something spoken by Zacharias, father of John the Baptist, is associated with the symbolism of the unicorn. "Blessed be the Lord God of Israel; for he hath visited and redeemed his people, And hath raised up an horn of salvation for us in the house of his servant David".

The *Physiologus* mentions another story about the unicorn. A snake poured its venom into a large lake and made it undrinkable. The other animals sensed the poison and did not dare to drink the water and instead awaited the arrival of the unicorn. It made the sign of the cross in the water with its horn, and so destroyed the poison. Once the unicorn had slaked its thirst, all the other animals did so, too.

Bodleian Library, Oxford.
Ms. Ashmole 1511, sheet 21r

Bodleian Library, Oxford.
Ms. Ashmole 1511, sheet 14v

Selected Bibliography

Anderson, Frank J., *An Illustrated History of the Herbals*, New York 1977

Behling, Lottlisa, *Die Pflanze in der mittelalterlichen Tafelmalerei*, Weimar 1957

Behling, Lottlisa, *Die Pflanzenwelt der mittelalterlichen Kathedralen*, Cologne/Graz 1964

Biedermann, Hans, *Medicina magica. Metaphysische Heilmethoden in spätantiken and mittelalterlichen Handschriften*, Graz 1972

Blunt, Wilfrid/Sandra Raphael, *The Illustrated Herbal*, London/New York 1979

Brunner, Karl, 'Virtuelle and wirkliche Welt. Umweltgeschichte als Mentalitätsgeschichte', in Konrad Spindler (Ed.), *Mensch und Natur im mittelalterlichen Europa. Archäologische, historische und naturwissenschaftliche Befunde* (Series of papers by the Akademie Friesach 4), Klagenfurt 1998, 327–344

Clark, Willene B./Meradith T. McMunn (Ed.), *Beasts and Birds of the Middle Ages. The Bestiary and Its Legacy*, Philadelphia 1989

Cogliati Arano, Luisa (Ed.), Schipperges, Heinrich, Schmitt, Wolfram (intro.), *Tacuinum Sanitatis. Das Buch der Gesundheit*, Munich 1976

Curtius, Ernst Robert, 'Rhetorische Naturschilderung im Mittelalter', in *Romanische Forschungen* 56 (1942), 219–256

Delisle, Léopold, 'Traités d'Hygiène du Moyen Âge', in *Journal des Savants* annual 1896, September, 518–540

Fischer, Hermann, *Mittelalterliche Pflanzenkunde*, Munich 1929

Ganzenmüller, Wilhelm, 'Das Naturgefühl im Mittelalter', in *Beiträge zur Kulturgeschichte des Mittelalters and der Renaissance* 18, Leipzig/Berlin 1914

George, Wilma/Brunsdon Yapp, *The Naming of the Beasts. Natural History in the Medieval Bestiary*, London 1991

Grape-Albers, Heide, *Spätantike Bilder aus der Welt des Arztes. Medizinische Bilderhandschriften der Spätantike und ihre mittelalterliche Überlieferung*, Wiesbaden 1977

Gurjewitsch, Aaron J., *Das Weltbild des mittelalterlichen Menschen*, Moscow 1972

Hassig, Debra, *Medieval Bestiaries. Text, Image, Ideology*, Cambridge 1995

Hassig, Debra (Ed.), *The Mark of the Beast. The Medieval Bestiary in Art, Life, and Literature*, New York/London 1999

Das Hausbuch der Cerruti. Nach der Handschrift in der Österreichischen Nationalbibliothek. Translated from the Latin and with an epilogue by Franz Unterkircher, Dortmund 1979

Heilmeyer, Marina, *The Language of Flowers: Symbols and Myths*, Munich/London/New York 2001

Henkel, Nikolaus, 'Studien zum Physiologus im Mittelalter', in *Hermaea* N. F. 38, Tübingen 1976

Von der gesunden Lebensweise. Nach dem alten Hausbuch der Familie Cerruti, Munich/Vienna/Zurich 1985

Lexikon des Mittelalters, vol. I, Munich/Zurich 1980, 72–80 (Bestiarium), *vol. V*, Munich/Zurich 1991, 1476–1480 (Herbal), *vol. VI*, Munich/Zurich 1993, 2117–2122 (Physiologus)

Lund, Cornelia, 'Bild and Text in mittelalterlichen Bestiarien', in Febel, Gisela/Georg Maag (Ed.), *Bestiarien im Spannungsfeld zwischen Mittelalter and Moderne*, Tübingen 1997, 62–74

McCulloch, Florence, *Medieval Latin and French Bestiaries* (University of North Carolina, Studies in the Romance Languages and Literatures 33), Chapel Hill 1960

Modersohn, Mechthild, 'Natura als Göttin im Mittelalter. Ikonographische Studien zu Darstellungen der personifizierten Natur' (Acta humaniora), Berlin 1997

Murray Jones, Peter, *Heilkunst des Mittelalters in illustrierten Handschriften*, Stuttgart 1999

Pächt, Otto, 'Early Italian Nature Studies and the Early Calendar Landscape', in *Journal of the Warburg and Courtauld Institutes* 13 (1950), 13–47

Pächt, Otto, 'Eine wiedergefundene Tacuinum-Sanitatis-Handschrift', in *Münchner Jahrbuch der bildenden Kunst* 3. F. 3/4 (1952/1953), 172–180

Payne, Ann, *Medieval Beasts*, London 1990

Der Physiologus. Translated and with an explanatory text by Otto Seel, Zurich/Munich [3]1976

Physiologus. Naturkunde in frühchristlicher Deutung, ed. by Ursula Treu, Hanau [3]1998

Physiologus Bernensis, unabridged facsimile edition of the Codex Bongarsianus 318 in the Burgerbibliothek Bern. Commentaries by Christoph von Steiger and Otto Homburger, Basel 1964

Reddig, Wolfgang F., *Bader, Medicus und Weise Frau. Wege und Erfolge der mittelalterlichen Heilkunst*, Munich 2000

Schipperges, Heinrich, *Der Garten der Gesundheit. Medizin im Mittelalter*, Munich/Zurich 1985

Schipperges, Heinrich, *Die Kranken im Mittelalter*, Munich 1990

Schlosser, Julius von, 'Ein veronesisches Bilderbuch und die höfische Kunst des XIV. Jahrhunderts', in *Jahrbuch der Kunsthistorischen Sammlungen des Allerhöchsten Kaiserhauses* 16 (1895), 144–230

Tacuinum sanitatis in Medicina, unabridged facsimile edition in original format of the Codex Vindobonensis series nova 2644 in the Austrian National Library. Commentary, introduction, transcription and German translation of the texts to the images by Franz Unterkircher; English translation by Heide Saxer and Charles H. Talbot (*Codices selecti*, Facsimile VI, Commentarium VI), Graz [2]1986

Theatrum Sanitatis. Twelve coloured miniatures from an Italian Renaissance manuscript. With an introduction by Marie Luise Kaschnitz, Baden-Baden 1947

Unterkircher, Franz, *Tiere, Glaube, Aberglaube. Die schönsten Miniaturen aus dem Bestiarium*, Graz 1986

Wickersheimer, Ernest, 'Les Tacuinum Sanitatis et leur traduction allemande par Michel Herr', in *Bibliothèque d'Humanisme et Renaissance* 12 (1950), 85–97

Zimmermann, Albert/Andreas Speer, (Eds.), 'Mensch and Natur im Mittelalter' (Miscellanea Mediaevalia 21/1–2), Berlin/New York 1991–1992

Index of Plates

N.B. The Latin names listed above may differ from those given in the texts, where the original spelling found in the manuscripts has been used.

Photographic Credits

Bayerische Staatsbibliothek, Munich, p. 17

The Bodleian Library, Oxford, pp. 11, 13, 85, 87, 89, 91, 93

The British Library, London, pp. 8, 14, 15, 16,

Burgerbibliothek, Bern, Gerhard Howald, pp. 71, 73, 75, 77, 79, 81, 83

Österreichische Nationalbibliothek, Vienna, pp. 7, 10, 12, 19, 20, 25, 27, 29, 31, 33, 35, 37, 39, 41, 43 and back cover (detail), 45, 47 and front cover (detail), 49, 51, 53, 55, 57, 59, 61, 63, 65, 67, 69